INTEGRATING NEUROCOUNSELING IN CLINICAL SUPERVISION

Integrating Neurocounseling in Clinical Supervision provides an indispensable framework for understanding supervision using neuroscience. Chapters explore a range of topics, from basic neuroanatomy to the complexities of the default mode network. Beginning with overviews of supervision and of common challenges and ethical concerns, the book presents five supervision models, allowing the supervisor to select the best fit for each supervisee and each question. By combining supervision theory, practical applications, discussion questions, and case studies and demonstrations, the authors prepare counselors to be more intentional about brain functions to increase the efficacy of supervision. New video demonstrations available on the companion website emphasize client outcomes for each of the five supervision models and one group counseling scenario, connecting directly to chapter content and demonstrating the major elements of each model.

Lori A. Russell-Chapin, PhD, LCPC, BCN, is a professor of counselor education at Bradley University and an award-winning teacher and researcher.

Theodore J. Chapin, PhD, LCP, LMFT, BCN, is president and clinical director of Chapin and Russell Associates, a counseling private practice; Resource Management Services, a consultation organization; and the Neurotherapy Institute of Central Illinois, a neurofeedback practice.

INTEGRATING NEUROCOUNSELING IN CLINICAL SUPERVISION

Strategies for Success

Lori A. Russell-Chapin and Theodore J. Chapin

Routledge
Taylor & Francis Group

NEW YORK AND LONDON

First published 2020
by Routledge
52 Vanderbilt Avenue, New York, NY 10017

and by Routledge
2 Park Square, Milton Park, Abingdon, Oxon, OX14 4RN

Routledge is an imprint of the Taylor & Francis Group, an informa business

© 2020 Lori A. Russell-Chapin and Theodore J. Chapin

Library of Congress Cataloging-in-Publication Data
A catalog record for this title has been requested

ISBN: 978-1-138-58793-9 (hbk)
ISBN: 978-1-138-58795-3 (pbk)
ISBN: 978-0-429-46965-7 (ebk)

Typeset in Caslon Pro
by codeMantra

Visit the companion website: www.routledge.com/cw/chapin

Contents

ABOUT THE AUTHORS

Dr. Lori A. Russell-Chapin is a Professor of Counselor Education in the Department of Leadership in Education, Nonprofits and Counseling at Bradley University in Peoria, Illinois. She earned her Ph.D. in Counselor Education from the University of Wyoming. She is an award-winning teacher and researcher at Bradley University. Currently Lori is co-director of the Center for Collaborative Brain Research, a partnership among Bradley University, OSF Saint Francis Medical Center, and the Illinois Neurological Center. Lori enjoys writing and has published and presented extensively in the local, regional, national, and international arenas. She is the author or co-author of eight books on practicum/internship, supervision, conflict resolution, grief and loss, neurofeedback and neurocounseling. Lori is licensed in the state of Illinois as a LCPC (IL), and holds several certifications such as the Certification in Mental Health Clinical Counseling (CMHCC), Approved Clinical Supervisor (ACS), and Board Certified in Neurofeedback (BCN). She teaches clinical graduate counseling courses and is passionate about her part-time private practice with husband, Dr. Ted Chapin. Dr. Russell-Chapin was named the American Mental Health Counseling Association (AMHCA's) national Linda Seligman Counselor Educator of the Year. Then in 2017 she was honored with the international American Counseling Association Garry R. Walz Trailblazer Award for her work with neurocounseling. In 2018 Lori was awarded the Teaching Excellence Award for the College of Education and Health Sciences.

Dr. Theodore J. Chapin is a licensed psychologist in the state of Illinois and a licensed marriage and family therapist. He earned his Ph.D. from

Marquette in Counseling. He is board certified in neurofeedback (BCN) and holds certifications in forensic examinations and employee assistance programs. Dr. Chapin is the president and clinical director of Chapin & Russell Associates, a counseling private practice, Resource Management Services, a consultation organization, and the Neurotherapy Institute of Central Illinois, a neurotherapy and neurofeedback practice. Ted leads a group of 14 counselors, social workers, and psychologists. He continues to research, write and publish articles, chapters and books on counseling, neurofeedback, and clinical supervision. Dr. Chapin presents locally, nationally, and internationally on similar areas. He enjoys working on parental allocation evaluations and mediations. The company was awarded the Better Business Bureau Torch Award for Business Integrity.

PREFACE

The Beginnings of This Supervision Text

This supervision book has taken on a life of its own. The reasons are numerous. The first occurred when a master counselor came to one of the textbook's authors, Lori, for supervision, with a look of total puzzlement on his face. His name was Bryan, and he began supervision before Lori could even ask, "What would you like to work on in supervision today?" He was shaking his head and exclaiming, "I don't know what to do with this fairly healthy client! For years I have been working with mostly chemically addicted male clients. Now I have a female, nonaddicted person who talks a lot, and I think I am lost in counseling. I haven't been lost in a long time."

Bryan showed Lori his tape, and the genesis for this book began. Lori realized then that the manner in which she had been doing supervision was effective and efficient for Bryan's male addicted clients, but it would not work for this client.

Bryan was kind enough, flexible enough, and confused enough to experiment with differing supervision styles. He and his client courageously consented to using one of their supervision sessions so Lori could demonstrate five different supervision approaches. In the end, Bryan was asked which approach met his and his client's supervision needs the most. His answer was surprising yet understandable. What Bryan needed was not the typical cognitive behavioral supervision session. His confidence had been tested with a new population. He was questioning many of his solid addiction counseling skills. Lori used all five supervision models with his same supervision question: "What am I doing wrong? She just keeps talking and I don't feel connected. I want to get her into process but it is too difficult."

Bryan discussed the benefits of each supervision model, but the approach that seemed to help Bryan the most this time and responded best to his need and supervision question was theoretic specific. By modeling back during this supervision session, a variation of an Empty Chair technique that Bryan tried to use with his client, Bryan realized that his skills can generalize from population to population and that he needed to relax. Bryan also concluded that supervision over the life span of a counseling career can keep helping professionals sharp and less stressed. Bryan and Lori's videotaping experience was the genesis for this book; it seemed natural to expand on this idea and format.

Another reason for this type of supervision book is that both authors, Lori and Ted, practice counseling privately in a group practice. Lori teaches full time at a private, Midwestern university, Bradley University, and is able to consult eight hours per week at their private practice. The supervision needs of private practitioners, agency and school counselors, and graduate students differ, but the need for a supervision book for all settings seemed apparent.

As the clinical supervision field continued to grow and change, the need for an updated version became even more evident. The *Diagnostic and Statistical Manual* went through major changes and evolved into the DSM-5, and the world of neuroimaging gave birth to neurocounseling, bridging brain and behavior. In this exciting new textbook, all six supervision demonstrations illustrate these changes, along with neurocounseling implications that are embedded into each chapter. The demonstrations along with transcripts can be located at the website.

The Benefits and Purpose of This Text

Therefore, this supervision textbook will provide a "one-stop shopping" approach for all users whereby the reader can review supervision theory, discover individual supervision style, read about five supervision approaches to clinical supervision, observe a demonstration of those approaches, watch an agency group supervision in action, and begin to integrate neurocounseling and the brain into the supervisory process. The demonstrations will not show the way to conduct supervision, but they will show the authors' interpretation and style of the clinical supervision approaches and group supervision. In the individual supervision sessions, Lori is the supervisor. In the group supervision session, Lori is the supervisee and Ted is the supervisor.

In the world of clinical supervision, there are excellent supervision resources explaining academic theory and skills. However, it became clear that there were several missing pieces in the supervision knowledge base. Nowhere were there demonstrations and hands-on materials to which supervisors, supervisees, and/or students from different settings could turn when they were lost in the supervisory therapeutic process. Nowhere was there a resource that could actually demonstrate the differing styles and approaches to clinical supervision. There are many wonderful books and manuals on supervision, but nowhere was there one resource where all this information was integrated in a comprehensive manner.

This textbook will also focus on individual and group supervision and offer a strong knowledge base about supervision. The information gained will aid supervisees and supervisors in growing at a faster pace and becoming more autonomous in their developmental journey as helping professionals. Additionally, supervision approaches that will assist the reader in becoming more versatile, knowledgeable, and flexible will be explored. The approaches are developed from unique philosophical frameworks underlying the supervision process. Practical examples from each approach will be offered.

Textbook Outcomes

The reader may also follow along with the supervision demonstration using transcripts from the supervisor and supervisee. These can be found on the book's companion website, which can be accessed at Routledge.com. In addition, each chapter will offer reflective exercises so the supervisor and supervisee can practice and expand and integrate supervision and neurocounseling outcomes.

By the time the reader reaches the end of this book, he or she will be able to answer these questions: What do I need from supervision? What is my supervision style? Why should supervision continue over the life span of a counseling career? How can a supervisor minimize some of the potentially harmful effects of psychological treatment for a supervisee? How does the brain and neurocounseling interact with supervision? Many additional questions will be answered as well. Each chapter has several reflection questions offered throughout the chapter topics. The more questions the reader is willing to complete, the more supervision information can be gleaned from each important supervision chapter.

Supervision Chapter Topics

The authors believe that the topics in each chapter are critical to the success of the supervisory process. In these chapters are direct and practical applications for the supervisee and the supervisor. *Chapter One, A Clarifying View of Supervision*, defines clinical counseling supervision and encourages helping professionals to see the overall benefits of supervision throughout the life span of the counseling career. The basic tenets and definitions correlate with the roles, qualities, expectations, and functions of the supervisor/supervisee. A Supervision Policy is presented as an essential component of a supervisory team. Basic neuroanatomy is explained.

Chapter Two, Obstacles to Effective Supervision, offers the optimal combination of four important supervisory factors. These factors include the supervisee, supervisor, the supervisory relationship, and the structural elements of supervision. This chapter explores each of these factors and the potential obstacles they present for effective supervision, and offers some suggestions on how these obstacles can either be avoided or appropriately managed should they arise. The importance of understanding potentially harmful effects of treatment is also emphasized. A Head Map of Function (Figure 2.1) is presented to help better understand brain location sites and functions that impact the supervisory process.

In *Chapter Three, Ethics in Counseling Supervision*, the entire focus is on the ethical practice of clinical supervision. Each section presents an ethical problem that could readily arise in any setting where mental health services are provided. The reader is presented the problem with a set of discussion questions encouraging further reflection on the particular ethical dilemma. A short summary of the relevant ethical guidelines is provided, followed by a suggested course of appropriate action. Better understanding the role of conflict and the prefrontal cortex is presented as this chapter's neurocounseling topic.

Chapter Four, Developmental Supervision Models, is the first of five chapters devoted to differing supervision models. The discussion begins by offering a common-factor approach to supervision, identifying common elements throughout all supervision models. The chapter then provides an overview of developmental models of supervision. Each of the supervision model chapters is formatted describing the Basic Tenet, When to Use, Supervisor's Emphasis and Goals, Supervisee Growth Areas, and Limitations. This chapter has the transcript and demonstration, the Case of Ella, demonstrating the Stoltenberg, McNeil, and Delworth Developmental Supervision Model. Ella is a master-level counselor who has spent the majority of her many decades in a hospital setting. Her Supervision Question is "When and how do I fit Dad into the picture, so she [client] can be comfortable? How do I get more information for this young woman?" The correlating neurocounseling topic for this chapter is the use of the Polyvagal Theory and social interactions.

Theoretical-Specific Supervision Models is the title for *Chapter Five*. This chapter focuses on the advantages and disadvantages of using theoretical-specific supervision models. The five different psychotherapy-based supervision models highlighted are Rogerian, Rational Emotive Therapy, Psychodynamic, Attachment, and Feminist supervision models. Each model is formatted with the same constructs of Basic Tenet, When to Use, Supervisor's Roles and Behaviors, Supervisor's Emphasis and Goals, Supervisee Growth Areas, and Limitations. Again, the transcription is included in this chapter for the supervision demonstration using a Psychodynamic Supervision Model and the Case of Brad. Brad is a master-level social worker with 30-plus years of counseling experience. His supervision question is, "Given the fact that I've taken a fairly traditional cognitive behavioral and wellness model and neurotherapy combined with a biofeedback model to address his issues, is there another theoretical approach that I can take that would be fresh for him and uh... maybe hook us into an area that we missed in regard to why he's relapsing?" The relevant neurocounseling topic for this chapter is a discussion of homeostatic plasticity, and what we all need to continue to build new neuronal pathways.

Chapter Six, Social Role Supervision Models, provides the benefit of identifying and emphasizing the varied roles and foci that supervisors need. These supervision models offer structure and interventions for both the supervisee and supervisor. The models also assist the supervisory process by emphasizing the importance of interpersonal communication skills used by the supervisee. Bernard's Discrimination Supervision Model, Holloway's Social Role Supervision Model, and Hawkins and Shohet's Social Role Supervision Model showcase this type of supervision, using the same format as in the previous chapters.

The new supervision demonstration in this chapter utilizes the Discrimination Supervision Model in the Case of Jason. This licensed, master-level counselor has extensive residential treatment experience. His Supervision Question is, "Because he's not coming in directly to work with OCD, but he's kind of bridging that gap here, how am I supposed to work to decide whether thinking and having those thoughts (suicide) that maybe I do, but I don't think I do, or are they two separate identities?" To follow along when viewing the supervision demonstration, there is a transcript of the entire session. The related neurocounseling topic is how the Default Mode Network (DMN) can assist in needed mind-wandering in supervision for processing and comprehension.

In *Chapter Seven, Integrated Models of Supervision*, the supervision models tend to be atheoretical and use concepts from other counseling theories that are needed by supervisees. Integrated Supervision Models are designed for those who work from multiple theoretical orientations. Two approaches toward developing an integrated model are technical eclecticism and theoretical integration. In this chapter the integrated Microcounseling Supervision Model (MSM) uses the same written format as previous chapters. MSM utilizes both technical eclecticism and theoretical integration. This model introduces a standardized approach to supervision offering the supervisee strengths and areas for improvement. The Counseling Interview Rating Form (CIRF) is the instrument created for assessment. Follow along using the chapter transcription for a demonstration of the Microcounseling Supervision Model, an integrated and competency-based supervision model in the Case of Andrea. She is a recent graduate with her license and is working in her first counseling agency position. Andrea's Supervision Question is "How can I engage him better in counseling, and how can I reach Lawrence so he can be more comfortable with me?" The neurocounseling implication of active listening and the brain is discussed.

Interpersonal Process Recall in *Chapter Eight* creates an example of a widely used supervision approach developed by Norm Kagan. When supervision sessions require digital recording of counseling interviews or conducting counseling sessions in an actual live observation setting, Interpersonal Process Recall (IPR) can be utilized. This supervision approach allows supervisees to safely analyze their thoughts and feelings about the counseling interview. The chapter is written in the same format as the above chapters, providing suggestions of possible supervisory IPR leads and questions.

Transcripts are provided for the supervision demonstration illustrating IPR in the Case of Beth. This supervisee is a master-level prepared high school counselor working with a large and diverse school population. She is completing her first year as a high school counselor and is a National Certified Counselor and waiting for her license as a professional counselor. Beth's Supervision Question is "How do I address this feeling of loss with her when so much of our time is spent focusing on her behaviors?" The neurocounseling topic in this chapter is how negative bias influences counseling and supervision especially when dealing with feedback.

Chapter Nine, Benefits of Group Supervision, outlines the purpose, the advantages of group supervision, and some limitations of this supervision model. It will also delineate a procedure that can be readily applied to many mental health settings. Special attention will be given to the facilitator's role and the many clinical issues that a group supervision session can address. The chapter closes with a brief review of some related but vitally important topics that will explore some of the following questions: Should participation in group supervision be voluntary or mandatory? Should mental health professionals be charged for supervision? What kind of documentation will the facilitator need to keep? How can a group handle an issue involving an impaired therapist? How does group supervision change in various work settings? When is group supervision just not enough? How do the parietal lobes work in group supervision?

The Group Supervision demonstration shows a typical bimonthly multidisciplinary, private practice supervision session where there is a designated supervisor and supervisees. However, just like group counseling, the focus on the supervisor changes, and the supervisees become an active part of the supervisory process and team. There are three unique cases presented during this session, ranging from grief and loss, to suicidal ideations, to loss of confidence. Each supervisee has a distinct supervision question. In this group session, Lori, who has been the supervisor in all the individual supervision demonstrations, is now a supervisee. A transcript of the group supervision session is included.

The final chapter is designed to bring closure to the supervision textbook by discussing numerous variables and new directions impacting the field of counseling supervision. *Chapter Ten, Future Directions in Supervision*, divides the chapter into distinct topics that may influence the future. The topics range from technology to brain research to gerontology to evidenced-based and competency-based practices. The need for a Professional Supervision Will is also discussed, and a sample is offered.

The Supervision Journey

Every year I ask each of my new graduate students this question: Did you choose the counseling profession or did the counseling profession choose you? It is a wonderful reflection question, and somewhere, I am sure, the answer lies in the middle of the continuum. The supervision journey has a different answer, however. Each of us in the counseling profession can choose supervision as a lifelong aspect of our counseling career.

I so enjoy being a trained and certified supervisor, but I thrive as a counselor, professor, and supervisor when I am the recipient of continued supervision. As I change and grow in my counseling skill level, so do my supervision needs. Even after all these years, I need and want continued supervision. My supervision journey continues to expand and become more complex. Therefore, regular supervision leaves me rejuvenated, wiser, and healthier. The following quote helps me better understand the need for supervision, for I know that each of us, whether a client, student, colleague, or counselor, has a special yearning for competency. Become a believer in lifelong supervision and observe what happens to your counseling and supervision skill set!

Every blade of grass has its Angel bending over and whispering, "Grow, grow."—The Talmud

ACKNOWLEDGMENTS

This book is dedicated to all of our supervisors who taught us compassionately how to counsel, teach, consult, and behave in a professional manner. Thank you for your wisdom. Your guidance and support make a world of difference.

A special thank you to the editorial staff at Routledge and especially to Anna Moore, our main editor, whose skills, dedication, and wisdom made this textbook a reality.

1
A Clarifying View of Supervision

Overview

The purpose of this chapter is to encourage helping professionals to see the overall benefits of supervision throughout the life span of the counseling career, value those benefits as a professional necessity, and eventually discover supervision approaches that fit their needs. The basic tenets and definitions of clinical counseling supervision will be presented, along with the roles, expectations, and functions of the supervisor/supervisee. Throughout the book the authors will also integrate the latest information on neurocounseling and its implications to the supervisory process.

Goals

- Understand the need for a holistic, integrative supervision book.
- Define supervision and its major components.
- Explain how clinical supervision is an integral part of professionalism.
- Identify brain structures and functions that impact clinical supervision.

Supervision Defined

Much like counseling theories, supervision approaches have many similarities and differences. Of course, the main goal is to act as a gatekeeper for the helping professions and assist in effective client outcomes. Moreover the similarities for all models include: supervisee learning and development, support for the emotional effects of the work, and managerial and ethical responsibilities (Simpson-Southward, Waller, & Hardy, 2017, p. 1228). Most supervision models/approaches also emphasize the importance of a healthy supervisee and supervisor relationship, stress the importance of feedback and communication, and have a variety of supervisor tasks and functions. Understanding the differing categories, tenets, and functions of supervision will expand your clinical supervision knowledge base, plus allow you more diversity and selection of needed supervision skills. Each category may have something to offer the supervisory team based upon the needs of the supervisee (Russell-Chapin, Sherman, & Ivey, 2016).

However, in a recent content analysis of 52 supervision models, many differences were discovered. Seventy-one supervisory elements unfolded with little consistency in the models. Most emphasized the development of the supervisees, and only half of the models focused on the client and outcomes. Some supervision models never even mentioned the evaluation process (Simpson-Southward et al., 2017).

It is the authors' intention of this book then to offer fundamental, standardized, and foundational elements for all supervision models, yet continue to allow the needed diversity of the unique supervision models. With that in mind, supervision is often defined concisely as an emotionally safe, distinctive approach and response to a supervisee's needs from an expert who has more experience (Russell-Chapin, Sherman & Ivey, 2016; Bernard & Goodyear, 2008). Haynes, Corey, and Moulton (2003) add that clinical supervision is a process using consistent observation and evaluation from a trained counseling professional that has a specialized body of knowledge and skill. In an earlier and classic citation, Bernard and Goodyear (2004) offered this definition:

> Supervision is an intervention provided by a senior member of a profession to a junior member or members of that same profession. This relationship is: evaluative, extends over time and has the simultaneous purposes of enhancing the professional functioning of the more junior person(s), monitoring the quality of professional services offered to clients that she, he or they see(s), and serving as a gatekeeper of those who are to enter a particular profession. (p. 8).

Discussion Questions #1:

1. What is your definition of supervision?

_____

_____

_____

_____

2. What do you believe the benefits of supervision might be for you?

_____

_____

_____

_____

The Process of Supervision

The supervisor will usually clarify and combine three processes through-out supervision: roles, expectations, and functions. The roles that are used will be dependent on the supervisee's needs. During an informal or formal assessment the supervisor may decide that the "hat" of the teacher, consultant, evaluator, and/or encourager is needed (Bernard & Goodyear, 1998).

Holloway and Carrol (1999) suggest that it is the supervision tasks and roles plus their functions of those tasks that equal the supervision process. In other words, when the roles and responsibilities of the supervisor are combined with the need of the counselor in training, then a supervision process has begun.

During every supervision session the expectations must be clarified. Initially knowing what is expected from each member of the supervisory team is essential. The perceptions of the supervisor and supervisee will continue to be shared throughout the lifetime of supervisory experience. The functions of supervision will vary based upon the supervisee's needs as well. The major responsibilities, though, are that of administration, education, and support. A typical supervisory opening question might be, "What do you need and want out of supervision today?" (Russell-Chapin & Ivey, 2004).

Still, another aspect of the supervisory process has to consider the method of delivery. These decisions may have more to do with the actual clinical settings as well as the accreditation of many of our helping professional associations such as the Council for Accreditation of Counseling and Related Educational Programs (CACREP) for counselor educators. CACREP (2015) stipulates that triadic supervision is needed for practicum students. Further discussion of group supervision will be written about in Chapter Nine on Group Supervision. Many community settings prefer and only have access to small group supervision, and yet there are still professionals who prefer the intimacy of individual supervision. With each delivery modality, there are unique challenges from offering the best type of corrective feedback to sufficient amount of time to cover caseloads to the importance of establishing group norms (Borders, Welfare, Sackett, & Cashwell, 2017; Luke & Diambra, 2017; Borders & Giordano, 2016).

Another essential mandate for a successful supervision experience is the proper documentation. In Appendix 1.A of this chapter are examples of practicum/internship contracts, logs, consent forms and evaluations. Many institutions already use these types of forms.

The next category of forms is not often required. These newer forms will be included in the body of the chapter for further reflection. Whether the supervisee is a graduate student or a practicing counseling professional some type of a clinical supervision policy and supervision plan is a must. Both the written supervision policy and the supervision plan assist in clarifying the expectations, tasks, and roles in the supervision relationship. The following policy example is one the authors use in their private practice.

Resource Management Services, Inc.

Clinical Supervision Policy
(Draft)

1. All professional staff are required to participate in clinical supervision. Staff may choose from two supervision formats, individual or group.

Group supervision will be provided twice a month (once a month in June, July and August), at no cost to staff. Individual supervision must be arranged privately. All staff are required to attend group supervision a minimum of two hours a month or individual supervision one hour a month. Any other arrangement must be approved by the group's Chief Clinical Supervisor (CCS), Ted Chapin, Ph.D. Check your professional association's supervision requirement to determine how much supervision you need. Pressing clinical issues that cannot wait for scheduled supervision, are to be brought to immediate supervisory attention.

2. All supervisory discussions will be appropriately documented and filed with the CCS. The documentation is to include the date, counselor name, client name, supervisory issue, recommended action and as indicated, resolution. In addition, the name of each person attending supervision will also be noted.

3. All clinical staff are expected to follow their respective professional ethical guidelines and are further required to give special attention to the following primary clinical duties, presenting any such issue for immediate supervision.

   a. Duty to prevent client from harming self or others.
   b. Duty to protect client confidentiality.
   c. Duty to provide for client continuity of service.
   d. Duty to keep adequate clinical records.
   e. Duty to properly diagnose and treat clients.
   f. Duty to avoid dual relationships and sexual impropriety.

   All office staff (clerical, accounting, data management, and administrative) must also as appropriate, follow and/or be mindful of the above primary duties, presenting any such issue to their immediate supervisor for feedback, clarification, and/or appropriate action.

4. All clinical staff are to make reasonable arrangements for their client's care should they be unavailable due to vacation or illness. This includes notification to the on-call person of clients who may be in crisis while you are not available and notice to clients who are in crisis, that you will not be available but an on-call staff will be available to help them. Any resulting incidents are to be appropriately

documented and forwarded to the primary therapist at earliest possible notice.

5. All clinical staff are required to complete a professional will that outlines the actions to be taken for the care of their clients, their records, and compensation due to you, should you become functionally incapacitated or deceased (see attached example).

6. All staff are covered for any professional acts of malpractice by the organization's liability insurance policy. This does not limit individual staff from maintaining their own liability policy at their own expense. Should any staff receive notice of a licensing board complaint or a potential legal action being filed, they should immediately apprise the CCS.

7. Finally, it is also understood that the clinical supervisor's role may include, as necessary, the audit of staff client records, review of staff client satisfaction surveys, assessment of staff clinical competency and investigation of complaints brought forward against an individual staff person. It is further understood that the primary intent of any oversight action will be to assess the situation, discuss the matter with the given staff person and resolve the presenting clinical problem.

Should the problem involve a more serious ethical infraction, the clinical supervisor may also require remedial action including but not limited to: continuing education, individual supervision, restriction or limitation of professional duties, report to the respective staff person's licensing board, and/or termination of employment. Staff may appeal any remedial requirement by submitting such a request in writing to the CCS. A panel of three colleagues, selected by the CCS, will review the appeal.

It is understood that the goal of the RMS Clinical Supervision Policy is to guard the quality and care of client treatment by supporting, monitoring and correcting any action that could be harmful to a client, jeopardize a staff person's professional standing, impede a supervisor's role, affect the group's reputation and standing in the community and/or present a risk of liability to individual staff members, clinical supervisors or the group practice. In this spirit, your signature below indicates your understanding, commitment to and compliance with the guidelines and requirements noted above.

_____, _____   _____, _____
Staff Signature   Date   Chief Clinical Supervisor   Date

If the supervisee is a graduate student some type of Internship Supervision Contract must be utilized. The forms at the end of this chapter are examples from a packet of information each intern is given in the graduate program at Bradley University. All of these forms provide structure and guidance for successfully engaging the supervisory process. See Appendix 1.A.

The Supervision Plan

The supervisee and supervisor can develop two plans, if needed. The first is a long-range plan spelling out long-term goals. The second supervision plan creates a format for individual supervision sessions. The formats can also be personally developed, however the following need to be included in the plans: supervision goals, expectations and question for each session, developmental needs of the client and supervisee, multicultural issues, diagnosis/conceptualization, evaluations, and supervision notes and outcomes (Russell-Chapin et al., 2016; Stoltenberg & Pace, 2008; Russell-Chapin, 2007).

Discussion Questions #2:

1. At this moment, what do you want out of your clinical supervision? Be sure to complete the Supervision Policy and Plan with your supervisor.

_____

_____

_____

2. What expectations need to be clarified to make the supervisory experience successful?

_____

_____

_____

Supervision Foundational Elements

Ellis (2006) conducted a research study using naturalistic data examining Loganbill, Hardy, and Delworth (1982) and Sansbury (1982) hierarchical model and found that supervisory relationship, competence, emotional awareness, and autonomy are essential variables for training supervisors. The authors concur with Ellis and additionally structure their supervision with six essential foundational elements that most supervision sessions must address: expectations, multicultural differences between the supervisor and supervisee, supervisory questions, selection of supervision approach dependent upon supervision question, diagnosis and conceptualization/interventions, and supervisory outcomes. Therefore these elements will be addressed and demonstrated throughout the text and video examples:

1. Clarify Supervision Expectations and Building Supervisory Relationships
2. Explore Multicultural Backgrounds; Similarities and Differences
3. Listen to Supervisory Questions
4. Select an Appropriate Supervision Approach
5. Discuss Diagnosis/conceptualization
6. Analyze supervisory outcomes.

Categories of Supervision

The two major categories of supervision are clinical and administrative. Although the functions of the categories often overlap, the focus of each is distinct. Clinical supervision emphasizes the services, direct and indirect, that a supervisee provides to clients. Clinical supervision usually means face-to-face supervision promoting supervisee development, working on counseling skills in the counseling relationship, advocating for the client's best interest, conceptualization, diagnosis and prognosis (Powell, 1993).

Administrative supervision has its focus on the roles and responsibilities that the supervisee must provide to the organization, agency, or employer (Tromski-Klingshirn & Davis, 2007; Bradley & Kottler, 2001). Tromski-Klingshirn (2006) stated that there are many role conflicts and role ambiguity issues when the same person is the clinical supervisor and the administrative supervisor. However in research by Tromski-Klingshirn (2006), 70 counselor supervisees who were working on the second tier of their state licensure responded to a study about dual supervisory roles. Forty-nine percent reported that their main clinical supervisor was also their administrative supervisor. Fifty-one percent stated that the primary clinical supervisor was not the administrative supervisor. After the data was analyzed no statistical group differences were found. Generally what supervisees thought about the dual roles tended to hover around the attributes and attitudes of the individuals involved in supervision, more than their roles.

In the world of the counselor this administrative aspect might have to be handled by the same person for the smooth functioning of the organization. It is the authors' opinion that, if possible, clinical supervision is still best achieved from a supervisor who does not have administrative and/or evaluative functions. The supervisee can then focus on honest fears and insecurities without concern of job performance, merit raises, and reprisals. Perhaps the best is a combination of supervision from within the organization and outside of the organization.

Supervision and Professionalism

All of the helping professions use some type of clinical supervision to assist students and helping professionals alike in developing new counseling skills, maintaining current skills, and building professional competencies (Haynes et al., 2003). The use of clinical supervision seems universal, but the manner in which professionals conduct supervision varies widely.

The counseling profession, like any discipline offering a public service, has a responsibility to assess continually the quality of the service. It is also the responsibility of the counselor to analyze the degree to which counseling is helping clients and its overall effectiveness and outcome (Nugent, 1990). As Neukrug (2003) so eloquently stated, "Embracing a professional lifestyle does not end once one finishes graduate school, obtains a job, becomes licensed, has ten years of experience or becomes a 'master' therapist. It is a lifelong commitment to a way of being, a way that says you are constantly striving to make yourself a better person and a more effective counselor, committed to professional activities" (p. 72).

Supervision Over the Life Span of a Counseling Career

Any supervisor and supervisee must have the supervision theory and skills to adjust to the needs of clients. For many years in the supervision world, that has not been the case. There has been a long-standing idea that good counselors make good supervisors. If the counselors understand the world of counseling, then they will understand the world of supervision. There are many problems with that assumption (Gazzola & Theriault, 2007). One problem is that relying on the counseling process to facilitate the supervision process may not be appropriate and could lead to damaging supervisory experiences (Ladany, 2004). Historically few supervisors have been trained in supervision. Without proper supervision training, many helping professionals often become comfortable and perhaps complacent and even safe in the views of how counseling and supervision should be accomplished.

The current view of supervision is that clinical supervision is emerging as a separate field of knowledge with a distinct skill set of theories, skills, and processes (Borders et al., 2014; Bernard & Goodyear, 2008). Another recent change is that one of the most exciting and fruitful methods of achieving the goal of becoming a seasoned helping professional is to engage in clinical supervision throughout the life span of a counseling career (Russell-Chapin et al., 2016; Grant & Schofield, 2007). For many counselors, clinical supervision began in graduate school, and once the program of study was completed, so did the days of supervision (Russell-Chapin, 2007). The material in this book will hopefully convince and encourage students, faculty, and helping professionals to understand the benefits of incorporating supervision across the life span of our counseling careers, whether that be as a supervisor, supervisee, or both.

Although there is a paucity of research studies that focus on supervision throughout the counseling career, Townend, Iannetta, and Freeston (2002) conducted a survey of 280 randomly selected members of the British Association of Behavioural and Cognitive Psychotherapists. Ninety percent of the sample met the supervision requirements of the association and were very satisfied with their supervisory experience. In England 72 percent of the 127 psychologists surveyed received postqualification supervision, but only 18 percent were satisfied with the supervisory arrangements (Gabbay, Kiemle, & Maguire, 1999). This trend may be changing, as clinical supervision research is gaining momentum, and the research is demonstrating more and more the necessity of supervision and its most effective practices (Borders et al., 2014).

Discussion Questions #3:

1. What are the benefits that you see from continuing supervision over the life span of a counseling career?

_____

_____

_____

2. What might the disadvantages be if supervision is not continued?

_____

_____

_____

Supervision Advocacy

Supervision advocacy is now in the forefront because many see the benefits of supervision over the lifespan of a career. Lori found this to be true in returning to supervision on her university sabbatical. Ted has always continued in supervision since he began practicing over 30 years ago. Supervision continues to refresh, rejuvenate, and keep us on the cutting edge. If more helping professions will view supervision as an ongoing cutting-edge practice, then the counseling profession will also become more accountable and outcome effective (Russell-Chapin, 2007).

The concept of supervision has changed over the years. Although supervision of counseling interns has always been a constant, now many helping professions are requiring supervision courses in their curricula and many state licensing boards are mandating that all renewing and newly licensed professionals have additional coursework in supervision.

As more helping professions understand the benefits of supervision over the lifespan of a counseling career, graduate curricula and state statutes governing licensure will continue to change and grow. In the state of Illinois, renewal of licensure now depends upon earning 18 contact hours of supervision training. When asked the reason behind this new requirement, the board stated that most of the grievances came about because of poor or inadequate supervision. As Lori has been conducting supervision workshops throughout the state and nation, she began collecting ideas from all the supervision experts and participants encountered. One of the first interactive group questions asked was, "What are the best and worst traits of the supervisors you have encountered?"

In Table 1.1 the readers can see the cumulative answers to this question. The following qualities seemed to be the main responses from approximately 500 supervisors and supervisees.

Table 1.1 Best and Worst Supervisor Traits

Best Supervisor Traits	Worst Supervisor Traits
Available	Blaming
Beside you (mentor)	Condescending
Calm and warm	Controlling
Caring	Critical
Challenging	Defensive
Collaborative	Distracted
Comfortable and positive	Distracting
Constructive feedback	Fear
Creative	Impaired
Developmental awareness	Inadequacy of skills
Empathized	Inappropriate jokes
Encouraging	Insensitivity
Equal	Lack of advice
Equal power	Lack of balance
Fun	Manipulative
Humble and wise	Micromanaged
Humor	Mismatched
Nonjudgmental	Narrow-minded
Options	No availability
Protects the profession	No feedback
Reciprocity	No listening
Resourceful	No options
Respectful	Non-engaging
"Saw the best in me"	Not flexible
Secure	Not validated
Shares ideas	Politics
Solid knowledge base	Snapped fingers
Strategic	Stereotypes
Suggestions	Too much trouble
Supportive	Too opinionated
Trust	Unethical
Validated	Unwelcoming

Introduction to the Individual and Group Supervision Video Demonstrations

Hi, My name is Dr. Lori Russell-Chapin, and I have been teaching and supervising graduate students at Bradley University in Peoria, Illinois, for the past 30 years. Last year I was on sabbatical, and I returned to a supervision group as a supervisee on a more regular basis. Once again what I discovered was that I enjoy being a supervisee as much as I love being a supervisor.

The concept of supervision has changed over the years. Now many helping professions are requiring supervision courses in their curricula and many state licensing boards are mandating that all licensed professionals have additional coursework in supervision. This new thinking arose out of several grievance procedures where poor supervision was being received.

Supervision advocacy is also in the forefront because many see the benefits of supervision over the life span of a career. I found this to be true in returning to supervision. Supervision continues to refresh, rejuvenate, and keep me on the cutting edge. If more helping professions will view supervision as an ongoing must, then the counseling profession will also become more accountable and outcome effective.

Viewers will have the opportunity to watch five individual case studies with five unique helping professionals who are at different points in their careers. Each case and counselor have differing needs and demands, so I will demonstrate five separate models of supervision that are relevant to the supervision needs. There is one group supervision demonstration as well.

The definition I am using for supervision is it is a distinct approach and response to supervisees' needs from a supervisor who often has more technical expertise and wisdom. The main goal is for viewers to understand that many unique supervision methods and models exist and that there is not one model that meets all of the supervision needs.

Observing six unique supervision models allows for much diversity and may help you to find a "best fit supervision model" for you based upon supervisory needs. Recognize that, though the models are different, I am demonstrating each model using the six foundational elements of: clarifying expectations, exploring differences between supervisor and supervisee, listening to the supervision question, selecting an appropriate supervision approach, discussing diagnosis/conceptualization, and analyzing supervisory outcomes.

Neurocounseling and Its Implications for Supervision

Functional magnetic resonance imaging (fMRI) research results have demonstrated that counseling changes the brain (Ivey, Bradford Ivey, & Zalaquett, 2017). If the same therapeutic relationship exists and many of the same counseling skills are used in supervision, then it makes sense that similar changes are occurring in the brain with clinical supervision. It is imperative that supervisors/supervisees understand the neurocounseling benefits of excellent supervision. Therefore, in this book and in each chapter there will be a relevant aspect of neurocounseling presented. In this chapter a general discussion of the brain and its functions will be addressed.

The Brain

This section is a compilation from the works of Thompson and Thompson (2003), Kershaw and Wade (2011), and Chapin and Russell-Chapin (2014). The human brain is the master organ controlling every function of our body. It contains over 100 billion neurons, weighs only about two and a half to three pounds and receives 20 percent of our cardiac output, 25 percent of our oxygen, and uses 25 percent of all the glucose available to our body. Its consistency is that of a soft boiled egg and it is precariously housed in a hard, protective skull often making it vulnerable to damage as in the case of concussion or closed head injuries. The brain is responsible for our behavior, affect, perception, cognition, and personality. It controls how our body responds to stress and disease. It's responsible for our body's physiological and emotional functioning, daily maintenance, decline, repair, and recovery. When all is going well our breathing, heart rate, body temperature, digestion, and affect promote health and a sense of well-being. When distressed, our breathing and heart rate increase, peripheral body temperature decreases, digestion slows, and affect becomes tense and reactive.

When properly functioning, our brain is self-regulating. It helps us navigate the demands of life allowing us to cycle as needed between states of calmness and alert.

However, prolonged exposure to distress or other sources of dysregulation can cause neurological instability resulting in impaired self-regulation. More specifically, the electrochemical functioning of our neurons can become imbalanced and our bodies can't function as designed. As a result we develop a variety of behavioral and emotional health problems related to the under-functioning and over-functioning of specific parts of our brain. For example, when we can't shut off the distressed response, we may develop an over-functioning, anxiety disorder. When we become exhausted, we may develop an under-functioning, depressive disorder. In addition, dysregulation can also occur when the normal communication pathways between neurons and brain structures or regions become disrupted.

The Brain and Neuroanatomy

The cerebral cortex, or the outer portion of the brain, integrates information from the sense organs, manages emotions, retains memory, and mediates thinking and emotional expression. It is divided into two hemispheres, the right and left, and is connected by the corpus callosum or neuronal fibers allowing communication between the hemispheres. Short fibers act as major roads connecting areas of the right and left hemispheres and long fibers act as superhighways allowing fast connection between areas. At the front of the corpus collosum is the cingulate gyrus. It is active in cognitive tasks, maintaining focus and problem solving. Problems with the cingulate gyrus involve obsessive thinking and compulsive behavior.

The right hemisphere is generally involved with social interaction, spontaneity, and aesthetic appreciation. More specifically, the right hemisphere helps to regulate attention, inhibit old habits, and sense the gestalt of an experience. It involves parallel processing, spatial relationships, the understanding of geometric forms, orientation in space, and holistic perception. It also plays a vital role in the emotional aspects of language through the processing of verbal intonation. Right hemisphere dominance is noted by distractibility, stimulus seeking, novelty, change, emotional involvement, extroversion, and an external locus of control. It is also related to histrionic tendencies, impulsiveness, and mania. It relies on an accommodating, fast and simultaneous style of information processing. Its dominant neurotransmitters are noradrenaline (speeding up action) and serotonin (slowing down action). Right hemisphere dominance is what we use for emotional processing and can be a source of problems with impulsivity, aggression, disinhibition, anxiety, and social interaction.

The left hemisphere is involved with language, writing, math, logical reasoning, and analytical, sequential processing. More specifically, it is the center for speech and syntax, writing, auditory verbal representation, object naming, word recall, visual imaging by auditory input, letter and word perception and recognition, abstract verbal formation, and perception of complex relationships. It also regulates attention, aids in inhibiting action and switching our responses and is the source of inner dialogue used to regulate behavior. Left hemisphere dominance is noted by a lack of emotions, introversion, goal-directed thinking and action, and an internal locus of control. It relies on an assimilative, slower style of serial processing. Its dominant neurotransmitter is dopamine (responsible for reward-driven behavior). Left hemisphere dominance is what is typically measured on an intelligence test and can be the source of problems with language, dyslexia, learning disorders, negative internal dialogue, and depression.

Each hemisphere is divided into four lobes. These are the frontal, temporal, parietal, and occipital lobes. The frontal lobes are responsible for our so-called executive functions. They help us plan for the future, anticipate consequences, analyze choices, learn and express language (Broca's area), and inhibit inappropriate or unwanted behavior. They also hold our personality, sense of self-confidence, independent judgment, willingness to take risks, and our extroverted or introverted nature. Persons with attention deficit hyperactivity disorder often have problems with their frontal lobes. Problems with the right frontal lobe often result in anxiety. Problems with the left, result in depression.

The temporal lobes assist with auditory processing, short-term or working memory, comprehension of word meaning (Wernicke area) and integration of new information, retrieval of words and the emotional valance of thoughts and behavior including temper control. They also organize our sense of hearing and smell. Problems with the left temporal lobe can involve aggression, violent thoughts, sensitivity to provocation, paranoia, decreased verbal memory, and emotional instability. Problems with the right temporal lobe can involve perception of melodies, meaning of verbal tone, social cues, and facial expression. It also involves social difficulty, problems processing music, distortion in visual and auditory memory, a sense of déjà vu and religious or moral preoccupation.

The parietal lobes are involved in integrating raw sensory information, perception of the physical body and motor functions including touch, pressure, temperature, taste, pain, spatial relations, and navigation. Problems with the parietal lobes include difficulty processing information, understanding directions, sensory sensitivity, physiological arousal, attention and hypervigilance.

The occipital lobes are responsible for visual processing, image construction, visual memory, and pattern recognition. Problems with the occipital lobes can involve impaired vision and difficulty dreaming. The occipital lobes have also been implicated in problems with post-traumatic stress disorder. So with every supervision skill that is demonstrated, a part of the brain will be activated in both the supervisor and supervisee.

Summary

This chapter focused on the manner in which you can use this textbook, a working definition of supervision, six foundational elements for all supervision models/approaches, and the impact of supervision over the life span of a helping professional career. Readers need to understand that many unique supervision methods and models exist that correspond to basic supervisee needs based on the supervisee's Supervision Question for every session. A major goal of this textbook is to assist helping professionals in expanding their knowledge base for supervision and discovering models of supervision that can allow them to respond more effectively and flexibly, whether the role is of supervisor and/or supervisee. This first chapter also offers several forms to assist in providing structure, expectations, and roles. The section of neurocounseling and its implications for supervision was discussed by offering general information about the brain and its structure and function.

Chapter One Final Discussion Questions:

1. Please answer the following question. Think back to your best and worst supervisory experiences in any work/life experience. What were the qualities of the best supervisors and worst supervisors? If your answers are not in the Chapter One table, be sure to write to Lori and Ted, so we can add your comments to the list.

_____

_____

_____

_____

2. As you write down your best supervisor qualities, a profile of a healthy supervisor begins to emerge. Are these the same supervisory traits that you see yourself exhibiting? Explore.

_____

_____

_____

_____

3. Why is it essential to better understand the brain and its functions and to incorporate neurocounseling into clinical supervision?

_____

_____

_____

References

Bernard, J.M. & Goodyear, R.K. (2008). *Fundamentals of clinical supervision* (4th ed.). Needham Heights, MA: Allyn & Bacon.

Bernard, J.M. & Goodyear, R.K. (2004). *Fundamentals of clinical supervision* (3rd ed.). Boston: Allyn & Bacon.

Bernard, J.M. & Goodyear, R.K. (1998). *Fundamentals of clinical supervision*. Needham Heights, MA: Allyn & Bacon.

Borders, L.D., Welfare, L.E., Sackett, C.R., & Cashwell, C.S. (2017). New supervisors' struggles and successes with corrective feedback. *Counselor Education and Supervision*, 56, 208–224. doi10.1002/ceas.12073

Borders, L.D. & Giordano, L.A. (2016). Confronting confrontation in clinical supervision: An analytical autoethnography. *Journal of Counseling & Development*, 94, 454–463. doi:10.1002/jcad.12104

Borders, L.D., Glosoff, H.L., Welfare, L.E., Hays, D.G., DeKruyf, L., Fernando, D.M., & Page, B. (2014). Best practices in clinical supervision: Evolution of a counseling specialty. *The Clinical Supervisor*, 33, 26–44. doi: 10.1080/07325223.2014.905225

Bradley, L.J. & Kottler, J.A. (2001). Overview of counselor supervision. In L.J. Bradley & N. Ladany (Eds.), *Counselor Supervision: Principles, process and practice* (3rd ed.). Philadelphia: Brunner-Routledge.

Chapin, T. & Russell-Chapin, L. (2014). *Introduction to neurotherapy and neurofeedback: Brain-based interventions for psychological and behavioral problems.* New York, NY: Routledge.

Council for Accreditation of Counseling and Related Educational Programs. (2015). *CACREP 2016 Standards.* Alexandria, VA: Author.

Ellis, M.V. (2006). Critical incidents in clinical supervision and in supervisor supervision: Assessing supervisory issues. *Training and Education in Professional Psychology*, S(2), 122–132.

Gabbay, M.B., Kiemle, G., & Maguire, C. (1999). Clinical supervision for clinical psychologists: Existing provision and unmet needs. *Clinical Psychology and Psychotherapy*, 6, 404–412.

Gazzola, N. & Theriault, A. (2007). Relational themes in counselling supervision: Broadening and narrowing processes. *Canadian Journal of Counselling*, 41(4), 228–243.

Grant, J. & Schofield, M. (2007). Career-long supervision: Patterns and perspectives. *British Association for Counselling and Psychotherapy*, 7(1), 3–11.

Haynes, R., Corey, G., & Moulton, P. (2003). *Clinical supervision in the helping professions: A practical guide.* Pacific Grove, CA: Brooks/Cole.

Holloway, E. & Carrol, M. (Eds.) (1999). *Training clinical supervisors: Strategies, methods and techniques.* London: Sage.

Ivey, A.E., Bradford Ivey, M., & Zalaquett, C. (2017). *Intentional interviewing and counseling: Facilitating client development in a multicultural society* (9th ed.). Boston: Cengage Learning.

Kershaw, C.J. & Wade, J.W. (2011). *Brain change therapy.* New York: Norton.

Ladany, N. (2004). Psychotherapy supervision: What lies beneath. *Psychotherapy Research*, 14, 1–19.

Loganbill, C., Hardy, E., & Delworth, U. (1982). Supervision: A conceptual model. *The Counseling Psychologist*, 10, 3–42.

Luke, C. & Diambra, J.F. (2017). Neuro-informed group work. In T. Fields, L. Jones & L.A. Russell-Chapin (Eds.), *Neurocounseling: Brain-based clinical approaches.* Alexandria, VA: American Counseling Association.

Neukrug, E. (2003). *The world of the counselor.* Pacific Grove, CA: Brooks/Cole-Thomson Learning.

Nugent, F. (1990). *An introduction to the profession of counseling.* Columbus, OH: Merrill Publishing.

Powell, D.J. (1993). *Clinical supervision in alcohol and drug abuse counseling: Principles, models, methods.* New York, NY: Lexington Books.

Russell-Chapin, L.A. (2007). Supervision: An essential for professional counselor development. In J. Gregoire & C.M. Jungers (Eds.), *The counselor's companion: What every beginning counselor needs to know.* (79–80). Mahwah, NJ: Lawrence Erlbaum.

Russell-Chapin, L.A., Sherman, N.E., & Ivey, A.E. (2016). *Your supervised practicum and internship: Field resources for turning theory into action* (2nd ed.). New York, NY: Routledge.

Russell-Chapin, L.A. & Ivey, A.E. (2004). *Your supervised practicum and internship: Field resources for turning theory into action.* Pacific Grove, CA: Brooks/Cole.

Sansbury, D.L. (1982). Developmental supervision from a skills perspective. *The Counseling Psychologist*, 10, 1, 53–57.

Simpson-Southward, C., Waller, G., & Hardy, G.E. (2017). How do we know what makes for "best practice" in clinical supervision for psychological therapists? A content analysis of supervisory models and approaches. *Journal of Psychology & Psychotherapy*, 24, 1228–1245.

Stoltenberg, C.D. & Pace, T.M. (2008). Science and practice in supervision: An evidenced-based practice in psychology approach. In W.B. Waldo (Ed.), *Biennial review of counseling psychology*. New York: Psychology Press.

Thompson, M. & Thompson, L. (2003). *The neurofeedback book: An introduction to basic concepts in applied psychophysiology*. Wheat Ridge, CO: Association for Applied Psychophysiology and Biofeedback.

Townend, M., Iannetta, K., & Freeston, M.H. (2002). Clinical supervision in practice: A survey of UK cognitive behavioural psychotherapists accredited by the BABCP. *Behavioural and Cognitive Psychother*apy, 30, 485–500.

Tromski-Klingshirn, D. (2006). Should the clinical supervisor be the administrative supervisor? *The Clinical Supervisor*, 25(1/2), 53–67.

Tromski-Klingshirn, D.M. & Davis, T.E. (2007). Supervisee's perceptions of their clinical supervision: A study of the dual role of clinical and administrative supervisor. *Counselor Education and Supervision*, 46, 294–304.

APPENDIX 1.A EXAMPLES OF PRACTICUM/INTERNSHIP CONTRACTS, ACTIVITIES, PROGRAM OF STUDY, CONSENT AND RELEASE FORMS, AND EVALUATION

PRACTICUM/INTERNSHIP CONTRACT

This agreement is made on _____ by and between
month/day/year

_____ and the Human Development Counseling
Field Site

Program at (institution). The agreement is effective for a period from

_____ to _____ for a minimum
month/day/year   month/day/year

of 750 clock hours. Hours worked during University holidays and breaks
will be determined by the student and site based on the needs of school
or agency.

The Human Development Counseling Program agrees:

1. to assign a University faculty liaison to facilitate communication between the University and the site.
2. to provide a profile of the student, an academic calendar, and a course syllabus for Practicum/Internship.
3. to notify the students that they must adhere to the administrative policies, rules, standards, schedules, and practices of the site.

4. that the faculty liaison shall be available for consultation with both site supervisors and students.
5. that the University supervisor is responsible for the assignment of a course grade.
6. that the student carries liability insurance in the amount of $1,000,000/ $3,000,000 during the entire time this agreement is in effect.

The Practicum/Internship site agrees:

1. to assign a practicum supervisor who has the appropriate credentials, time, and interest for training the student.
2. to provide opportunities for the student to engage in a variety of counseling activities under supervision and for evaluating the student's performance.
3. to provide the student with adequate work space, telephone, office supplies and staff to conduct professional activities.
4. to provide supervisory contact which involves some examination of student work using audio/video tapes and observations.
5. to provide written evaluation of student's work based on criteria established by the University Program.

Name   Address   Phone   SS#

will be the primary site supervisor. The training activities checked below will be provided in sufficient amounts to allow an adequate evaluation of the student's level of competence in each activity.

Name   Phone

will be the faculty liaison with whom the student and practicum site supervisor will communicate regarding progress, problems, and performance evaluation.

PRACTICUM/INTERNSHIP ACTIVITIES

_____ Individual Counseling
personal/social/educational/
  occupational

_____ Career Counseling

_____ Group Counseling
co-leading
leading

_____ Supervision
individual
group
peer

_____ Intake Interviewing

_____ Case Conferences
staff meetings

_____ Testing
administration
analysis/interpretation

_____ Psychoeducational
Activities
parent conferences
outreach programs
inservices

_____ Consultation

_____   _____
Site Supervisor   Date

(Institution)
Program of Study

WEEKLY TIME SCHEDULE   WEEK #

* = Direct Service Hours

Date	Location Activity	Amount of Time* Comments	Practicum/Internship
_____	_____	_____	_____
		_____	
_____	_____	_____	_____
		_____	
_____	_____	_____	_____
		_____	
_____	_____	_____	_____
		_____	
_____	_____	_____	_____
		_____	
_____	_____	_____	_____
		_____	
_____	_____	_____	_____
		_____	
_____	_____	_____	_____
		_____	
_____	_____	_____	_____
		_____	

_____ _____ _____ _____

_____

_____ _____ _____ _____

_____

TOTALS:

This Week: Semester:

Total Hours: _____   Total Hours: _____

Direct Service Total: _____   Direct Service Total: _____

Client Informed Consent Form

I _____ agree to be counseled by a practicum/intern student in the (Program) at (Institution). I further understand that I may participate in counseling interviews that will be audio taped, video taped, and/or viewed by practicum/intern students through the use of one-way observation windows. I understand that I will be counseled by a graduate student who has completed advanced course work in counseling. I understand that the student will be supervised by a faculty member of the (Institution) (Program) and an agency site supervisor.

Client's Signature: _____

Date of Birth: _____ Today's Date: _____

Counselor's Signature: _____

Effective Date: _____

Expiration Date: _____

Client Release Form

I agree for my child, _____, to be counseled during the (date) school year by _____, Counselor Intern in the (Program) at (Institution). I understand that my child may participate in counseling interviews that may be audio taped or video taped, and/or viewed by practicum/internship students through the use of one-way observation windows. I further understand that _____ has completed advanced coursework in counseling/therapy and will counsel my child. I further understand that a (Institution) Professor and an on-site (Institution) supervisor will oversee the Counselor Intern.

_____ I agree for my child to be counseled by the Counselor
(date)   Intern for the school year and for those sessions to be video taped or audio taped.

_____ I agree for my child to be counseled by the Counselor
(date)   Intern for the school year; however, I do not wish for those sessions to be video taped or audio taped.

_____ I agree to have counseling information shared with:

_____

Person(s)

Parent/Guardian Signature _____ Date _____
Student Signature _____
Counselor Intern Signature _____ Date _____
Date Effective _____ Date Contract Expires _____

SITE SUPERVISOR'S EVALUATION OF STUDENT COUNSELOR'S PERFORMANCE

SUGGESTED USE: This form is to be used to evaluate overall performance in counseling. The form will be completed twice per term by the on-site supervisor. The form is appropriate for individual or group counseling.

Name of Student Counselor: _____

Name of Supervisor/Agency: _____

Date of Evaluation: _____

Period Covered by the Evaluation: _____

DIRECTIONS: The supervisor is to circle the number which best evaluates student counselor performance in each category.

General Supervision Comments	Requires Assistance	Appropriate Acceptable Performance	Exceptional Performance
1. Demonstrates a personal commitment in developing professional competencies	1 2	3 4	5 6
2. Invests time and energy in becoming a counselor	1 2	3 4	5 6
3. Accepts and uses constructive criticism to enhance selfdevelopment and counseling skills	1 2	3 4	5 6
4. Engages in open, comfortable, and clear communication with peers and supervisors	1 2	3 4	5 6
5. Recognizes own competencies and skills and shares these with peers and supervisors	1 2	3 4	5 6

6.	Recognizes own deficiencies and actively works to overcome them with peers and supervisors	1	2	3	4	5	6
7.	Completes case reports and records punctually and conscientiously	1	2	3	4	5	6

The Counseling Process

8.	Researches the referral prior to the first interview	1	2	3	4	5	6
9.	Keeps appointments on time	1	2	3	4	5	6
10.	Begins the interview smoothly	1	2	3	4	5	6
11.	Explains the nature and objectives of counseling when appropriate	1	2	3	4	5	6
12.	Is relaxed and comfortable in the interview	1	2	3	4	5	6
13.	Communicates interest in and acceptance of the client.	1	2	3	4	5	6
14.	Facilitates client expression of concerns and feelings	1	2	3	4	5	6
15.	Focuses on the content of the client's problem	1	2	3	4	5	6
16.	Recognizes and resists manipulation by the client	1	2	3	4	5	6
17.	Recognizes and addresses positive affect of the client	1	2	3	4	5	6

18.	Recognizes and addresses negative affect of the client	1	2	3	4	5	6
19.	Is spontaneous in the interview	1	2	3	4	5	6
20.	Uses silence effectively in the interview	1	2	3	4	5	6
21.	Is aware of own feelings in the counseling session	1	2	3	4	5	6
22.	Communicates own feelings to the client when appropriate	1	2	3	4	5	6
23.	Recognizes and skillfully interprets the client's covert messages	1	2	3	4	5	6
24.	Facilitates realistic goalsetting with the client	1	2	3	4	5	6
25.	Encourages appropriate actionstep planning with the client	1	2	3	4	5	6
26.	Employs judgment in the timing and use of different techniques	1	2	3	4	5	6
27.	Initiates periodic evaluation of goals, actionsteps, and process during counseling	1	2	3	4	5	6
28.	Explains, administers, and interprets tests correctly	1	2	3	4	5	6
29.	Terminates the interview smoothly	1	2	3	4	5	6

The Conceptualization Process

30. Focuses on specific behaviors and their consequences, implications, and contingencies.	1 2	3 4	5 6
31. Recognizes and pursues discrepancies and meaning of inconsistent information	1 2	3 4	5 6
32. Uses relevant case data in planning both immediate and longrange goals	1 2	3 4	5 6
33. Uses relevant case data in considering various strategies and their implication	1 2	3 4	5 6
34. Bases decisions on a theoretically sound and consistent rationale of human behavior	1 2	3 4	5 6
35. Is perceptive in evaluating the effects of own counseling techniques	1 2	3 4	5 6
36. Demonstrates ethical behavior in the counseling activity and case management	1 2	3 4	5 6

Additional comments/suggestions to improve performance:

_____

_____

_____

_____

_____

_____

_____

Date: _____   Signature of Supervisor: _____

My signature indicates that I have read the above report and have discussed the content with my site supervisor. It does not necessarily indicate that I agree with the report in part or in whole.

Date: _____   Signature of Student Counselor: _____

2
OBSTACLES TO EFFECTIVE SUPERVISION

Overview

Effective supervision can be viewed as an optimal combination of four important factors. These factors include the supervisee, supervisor, the supervisory relationship, and the structural elements of supervision. The supervisee brings with them a set of personal and professional needs as well as a capacity or readiness to benefit from the supervisory experience. The supervisor brings a set of abilities, skills, experience, and knowledge that prepares them to function as an effective mentor. The supervisory relationship involves the quality of match between the supervisee and supervisor. It is initially formed through careful pre-supervision selection and screening and is enhanced by the creation of a healthy supervisory chemistry. The relationship factor, or working alliance, is one of the few elements that all supervision models agree is of primary significance for effective supervision (Holloway, 1995; Morgan & Sprenkle, 2007). Although more subtle, the structural aspects of the supervision setting, such as available equipment, facility constraints, and professional staff support, are also important.

The purpose of this chapter is to explore each of these factors, the potential obstacles they present for effective supervision, and to offer some suggestions on how these obstacles can either be avoided or appropriately managed should they arise. The reader may find that some of the following issues will bring to mind other potential obstacles that are not fully addressed in this chapter. Should that occur, the principles outlined here may provide a helpful guide for how these, too, can be successfully resolved.

Inman et al. (2014) summarized the literature on the overall relevance of and access to clinical supervision. They concluded that while supervision is important in counselors' professional development it was, "disconcerting to see that many supervisees seem to have inadequate to no supervision despite regulations and ethical mandates" (p. 64). This is a troubling statement for it suggests that while educational programs do emphasize the value of supervision, once matriculated from these settings, mental health professionals encounter many obstacles in engaging ongoing supervision.

Goals

- Identify potential obstacles towards effective supervision.
- Offer resources to counteract obstacles.
- Assess one's personal supervisory preferences.

Supervisee Factors

Preparation: Supervisees enter supervision from a variety of preparation levels, and they bring their own opportunities and potential obstacles. Some supervisees are students. They typically have little experience, much excitement, some idealism and lots of anxiety. In the middle of the spectrum are new or junior professionals. They have some experience and are likely looking to fulfill qualifications for licensure or certification. They often bring more preconceptions about therapy and supervision and their expectations are often more well formed than students'. At the far end of the spectrum are experienced, senior professionals who very frequently have a clear idea of what they want out of supervision. They may be more focused and thus short-sighted about the range of possible benefits supervision can provide.

On a more behavioral level, a very real obstacle to supervision is a supervisee's lack of preparation for the supervision session. Did the supervisees take time to review their caseload, select a case for review, write up a thorough case summary report, decide how they were struggling, and conclude what they wanted supervision to address? Ironically, students, although less experienced, are often more disciplined in preparing for supervision than their more experienced counterparts. Their academic programs have often demanded that they organize their work and this has created a more disciplined approach to preparation. More experienced, employed professionals are frequently fitting supervision into their busy schedules. They often have a more focused agenda for supervision such as a particular client they are struggling with, a question about diagnosis, intervention ideas, or medication issues. Lack of thorough preparation will likely limit the supervisor's ability to offer a helpful response. It is one of the supervisor's responsibilities to formulate and communicate, early in supervision, a mutually agreed-upon set of supervisory guidelines and expectations.

Confidence: While student supervisees are obviously learning and acquiring their professional confidence, this may become limited by their reluctance to take appropriate risks and openly disclose to their supervisor. For example, perhaps they suspect a client may be suicidal but are afraid to ask, so they don't ask. In supervision the issue surfaces but the supervisee avoids expressing their concern with the supervisor. The opportunity for deeper learning is missed. With more experienced supervisees, lack of confidence or unwillingness to take appropriate risks may cause them to avoid developing new skills or trying a new intervention technique.

When a supervisee has negative reactions to their supervisor, they become even more reluctant to make appropriate disclosures to their supervisor (Inman et al., 2014). This creates obvious problems in both the supervisory relationship and the benefit of supervision for the supervisee and their client. Without open disclosure important questions go unaddressed and vital feedback and learning is lost.

Effective supervision for more experienced professionals is not only about fulfilling credentialing or licensing requirements or maintaining the status quo, it's also about the value of a supportive professional relationship and continued growth and professional development. The supervisory relationship provides a potentially rich environment for learning, application, and feedback. If professional counselors cannot stretch their skills in supervision or trust their supervisor, will they have the opportunity to enrich their professional competence?

Defensiveness: The word, supervision, in our culture has become synonymous with evaluation; evaluation can be intimidating (Russell-Chapin, Sherman, & Ivey, 2016; Russell-Chapin & Ivey, 2004). There is an obvious level of vulnerability present in the supervisory relationship, especially when a student supervisee works with an experienced senior clinician. This vulnerability, however, is also present when a senior professional works with a supervisor they consider their colleague. "If I disclose my flaws or shortcomings to this colleague, what will they think of me?" Sometimes, even asking a question can become an admission of doubt or a notice of something lacking. Defensiveness can become a serious obstacle to effective supervision.

Underlying defensiveness is insecurity, mistrust, and the lack of self-awareness. While most supervisees will bring to supervision their personal level of security or insecurity, mistrust will become magnified if the supervisory relationship becomes a place of humiliation or judgment. It is very important for supervision to be a safe place to explore self-doubt, take appropriate risks, be open to feedback, and learn from experience. This requires the supervisee to trust, to self-disclose, to listen, to become self-aware and react non-defensively to feedback. Inman et al. (2014) noted that supervisees who make the best use of supervision have greater cognitive complexity and self-awareness or reflectivity. Hill, Crowe, and Gonsalvez (2015), using thematic analysis of supervisees' reflections and feedback, found increased reflectivity led to discussion of supervisee anxiety, intentions to alter the supervisory role, identification of parallel process (dynamic transmission of relationship patterns between therapy and supervision), and improvements of the supervisory alliance.

Reduction of supervisee defensiveness also requires the supervisor to be empathetic, reassuring, and encouraging. This does not mean avoiding difficult conversations, but rather handling them in an honest, direct, genuine, and caring manner. This will allow the supervisee to comfortably face their insecurity and the supervisor to fulfill their obligation toward the competent practice of the profession. If resistance continues to grow, Backlund and Johnson (2018) suggest to go with the resistance and reframe as curiosity and healthy normal behavior using some basic motivational interviewing techniques.

Another method for decreasing the power differential between the supervisee and supervisor is to offer the supervisee the opportunity to openly discuss the supervisory experience and to evaluate the supervisor. Usually evaluation tends to be one-sided. The supervisee understands that he/she will be evaluated, but Downs (2000) suggested providing continuous evaluation of the supervisor may heighten the supervisee's investment in the supervision process and decrease anxiety.

Unresolved Personal Issues: One of the most difficult but one of the most important and powerful issues to face in supervision is when unresolved supervisee personal issues make themselves obvious in a counseling relationship. Some of these include therapists with anxious attachment styles (Beutler, Blatt, Alimohamed, Levi, & Angtuaco, 2006) or personal hostility (Henry, Strupp, Butler, Schacht, & Binder, 1993) that may impede therapeutic empathy. Other therapist vulnerabilities may include an excessive need to be liked or admired, an inability to receive criticism (Wolberg, 1967), difficulty tolerating negative emotion (Strupp & Hadley, 1985), and problems admitting and correcting errors committed during treatment (Greenson, 1967).

It takes a level of assertive confidence for the supervisor to address difficult issues, and it takes humility for the supervisee to acknowledge them. Left unaddressed, they can become the, "pink elephant in the living room" that everyone sees but dare not talk about. Ethically counselors usually understand their limits in being able to help a client when they themselves are struggling, perhaps unsuccessfully, with the same issue. Counselors may become hand-tied by their blind spots, biased positions, and limited ability to consider an alternate response. It is important for counselors to attend to unresolved personal issues and this may require the supervisee to seek personal counseling and/or limit their work with this type of problem until they are better able to address it with their clients. If the supervisee is impaired and could do or has done harm to clients, then appropriate action must take place.

Rapisarda and Britton (2007) conducted a qualitative study regarding the efficacy of sanctioned supervision for the impaired counselor. The results of their focus groups showed promise for the effectiveness of sanctioned supervision, if necessary remedial training for supervisors is also provided. They noted that the counseling profession has recognized the importance of identifying and intervening when counselors may be providing substandard care. Without exception, professional counseling organizations support intervention in cases of counselor impairment as detailed in their ethical guidelines (American Counseling Association, 2014; American Mental Health Counselors Association, 2015; American Psychological Association, 2017; and National Association of Social Workers, 2017). Following these standards both directs appropriate action for the therapist and supervisor, and protects clients' welfare.

Several recommendations to help impaired helping professionals include: advocating for lifelong supervision, encouraging supervisors to be gatekeepers of the counseling profession, emphasizing the importance of wellness and stress reduction, supporting supervisors who take action on subquality counseling and increasing evaluation and research efforts in the area of counselor impairment (Russell-Chapin, 2007; Cobia & Pipes, 2002; Thomas, 2005).

The supervisory role in the case of counselor impairment is to be supportive yet firm. The supervisor must set the boundaries regarding appropriate behavior and the supervisee must be willing to get help with their unresolved personal issue. This is not a problem to be addressed with shame or self-doubt but rather responsible action that will strengthen the supervisee personally and professionally enhance his or her competency.

Wellness and Compassion Fatigue: Increased attention has been given to counselors' health and wellness both while in training and as practicing professionals (Meany-Walen, Davis-Gage, & Lindo, 2016). This focus on self-care has obvious benefits for the supervisee and their clients. Integrating cognitive, emotional, physical, and spiritual dimensions toward optimal health has provided the foundation for wellness models of supervision (Lenz et al., 2012). Through education in wellness models and activities, and continuous use of wellness assessments, trainees and professionals can more readily develop their own wellness plan, better manage their health, and fend off problems of burnout and compassion fatigue often present in the helping professions. A therapist cannot function at their best without guarding against the exhaustion and fatigue, inevitable in assisting clients frequently in distress (Merriman, 2015). Protective factors and self-care plans learned in academic supervision and carried into professional practice can significantly reduce this occupational hazard.

Discussion Question #1:

Of the supervisee factors listed above, which one(s) may present the most difficult obstacle toward your effective supervision?

_____

_____

_____

_____

Supervisor Factors

The transition from supervisee to supervisor can be very challenging. Rapisarda, Desmind, and Nelson (2011) found two key factors involved in this process. These were establishment of a safe environment for supervisees and development of a supervisory skill set. The following factors will describe in more detail the necessary conditions a supervisor must provide for supervisee growth.

Competency: The first and perhaps most critical supervisor factor is the supervisor's training and competence in providing effective supervision. There are many ways that a supervisor can develop their competence. Supervisors can take formal graduate coursework in clinical supervision from an accredited institution. This will typically expose them to supervision theory and practice. Supervisors can also receive supervision of their supervision from an experienced and qualified colleague who has established credentials in the supervision of supervision. Another path to competency involves the attendance of professional workshops or seminars on clinical supervision. Many states now require 18 or more contact hours in supervision continuing education for renewal of state licenses. Finally, the Center for Credentialing and Education (CCE, 2019) offers an Approved Clinical Supervisor (ACS) certification. This involves completion of an application, a processing fee, and submission and review of an audio/video case presentation with multi-axial diagnosis. Inman et al. (2014) noted that a combination of formal training and supervised supervision promoted the development of a strong supervisor identity.

Nonspecific Feedback: Supervision between colleagues is a very useful and often convenient means of clinical supervision. However, in some situations, strong mutual interests in maintaining a respectful and friendly professional relationship can mute effective collegial supervision. This bind can potentially place the friendship above focused supervision and result in feedback that may be too general, vague, and not specific enough to be of any meaningful help to the supervisee. It is important supervisors feel free and able to give the quality and depth of feedback that will help the supervisee improve their skills.

A specific type of supervisee feedback involves the use of client feedback in supervision. Reese, Toland, and Slone (2010), working with psychotherapy trainees, found that those provided client feedback improved more than those who did not receive client feedback. While there was no difference in supervisory alliance or satisfaction with supervision, both therapist self-efficacy and client outcomes improved. Specific feedback provides more tangible information for therapeutic adjustments and client benefit.

Narrow Scope of Supervision: Some supervisors have a narrowly defined definition of supervision that significantly limits the supervisory opportunity for the supervisee. Sometimes supervision is limited to case conceptualization, diagnosis, and treatment planning. While useful, this does not address the myriad of issues that could be explored in supervision. Some of these include: enhancement of micro skills, the therapeutic relationship, theoretically based insights, self in the counseling process, transference and countertransference issues, projection, parallel process, alternative interventions, potentially harmful effects of treatment, ethics, and referral options. Two additional and potentially difficult supervisory issues involve sexual attraction and the integration of religion and spirituality in supervision.

Supervisee feelings of sexual attraction toward a client are seldom brought up during supervision. McMurtery, Webb, and Arnold (2011) suggested that the reason has to do with supervisors feeling hesitant due to concern about the blurring of professional and personal boundaries, and possible ethical complaints that could emerge from such sensitive conversations. While difficult to navigate, sexual attraction in therapeutic relationships is not uncommon and is an obvious focus for supervisory reflection and discussion. Also sensitive, are issues of religion and spirituality. Adams et al. (2015) noted that these issues are inconsistently addressed in counselor education due to lack of information about religion and spirituality, and lack of personal interest or perceived relevance to the primary therapeutic task. Of course issues of religion and spirituality can be very relevant to both the supervisory process and the counseling relationship. They involve diversity, respect for individual differences, and influence the obvious and subtle values of supervisees and clients. As such they are important matters for discussion in supervision.

Of course it is primarily up to the supervisor to manage the supervision session in such a way that these issues have an opportunity to be addressed. By expanding the scope of supervision, the supervisee will be more fully trained and prepared to offer effective clinical services to their clients.

In order to expand the scope of supervision, the norms and expectations of supervision must also expand. Supervision must promote both clinical competency and therapist personal growth. In so doing both the profession and consumer benefit. The counseling profession takes seriously its obligation for monitoring and preserving quality practice (Crocket, 2007; Falender & Shafranske, 2004; Feltham, 2000). Interest in expanding the scope of supervision has extended beyond the United States to include our European colleagues (West & Clark, 2004; Besley & Edwards, 2005).

Excessive Confrontation: When a supervisee enters each supervision session they are taking a risk in exposing their clinical limitations and, sometimes, sensitive personal issues. If a supervisor is too harsh, too confrontational, too critical, or too punitive in their style of feedback, the supervisee will likely feel threatened and withdraw. To support a supervisee's developmental growth, Borders and Giordano (2016) found that several steps in the confrontation process were needed. These included validating the supervisee, modeling effective confrontation skills, refocusing back to the client's experience, practicing the verbal delivery, offering encouragement, and remaining calm. The challenge for the supervisor is to be direct, focused, and encouraging so that the confrontation is delivered and the supervisee feels validated. While the content of supervision must be addressed, the supervisory relationship or working alliance also requires much attention or the entire supervisory process will break down.

Discussion Question #2:

Of the supervisor factors listed above, which one(s) will be the most important for you as the supervisor or supervisee?

_____

_____

_____

_____

Supervisory Relationship

The supervisory relationship or working alliance has been recognized as the most researched aspect of clinical supervision (Inman et al., 2014). Early on, Bernard (1979) in the Discrimination Model of Supervision, described the major roles of the supervisor as teacher, counselor, and consultant, and the major focus of supervision to involve intervention skills, case conceptualization, and personalization or attention to how the supervisee's personal issues and feelings may influence the therapeutic process. The task of building a strong supervisory relationship is complex and presents the potential for encountering many obstacles along the way. These can become evident through the sense of a tenuous relationship, frequent miscommunications, perceived lack of support, and inappropriate or disrespectful supervisory behavior (Inman et al., 2014). Overcoming these obstacles can strengthen the working alliance, especially when the supervisor can attend to the conflicts in an empathetic and nondefensive manner, be aware of their own limitations, model openness, and create a safe environment for genuine dialogue and learning (Nelson et al., 2008).

Personality Conflicts: While great effort is usually exercised in the formation of a good supervisory relationship, sometimes differences in personality undermine the essential development of rapport between a supervisor and supervisee. "The evaluative nature and disproportionate power inherent in the supervisory relationship make conflict in supervision a common reality" (Inman et al., 2014, p. 71). If attempts to overcome these differences fail, the supervisory relationship is bound to suffer and little effective supervision can be done (Fall & Sutton, 2004). While personality conflicts can disrupt the supervisory process, they can also present an opportunity for great learning and growth. By working through these differences, the supervisee and supervisor will likely be more effective in working with their own diverse client base. As therapists, it is not possible to like every client who comes through the door. It is, however, possible to learn how to work with different personality types. If not, the scope of a counselor's clinical practice will be severely limited. As in therapy, personality conflicts in clinical supervision can also significantly diminish the supervisory relationship. Research on the positive influence of supervisee and supervisor emotional intelligence (EQ) on a strong supervisory working alliance, suggests that coaching to enhance EQ may help to avert or decrease these conflicts (Cooper & Ng, 2009). However, when overwhelming, the option to end the supervisory relationship must also be considered. This is a challenging task but may ultimately result in a more complementary blend of personalities in the next supervisory relationship.

Mismatch of Theoretical Orientations: The theoretical orientations of professional counselors vary by training, supervision, and personal preference. Many theoretical orientations are anchored in time and through historical popularity. For example a Rogerian-oriented therapist may have been trained in the 1960s, a strategic therapist may have been trained in the 1990s, and a cognitive behavioral therapist trained in the 2000s. All bring a very distinct set of assumptions about the process and mechanisms of change, some of which are likely at sharp odds with one another. A mismatch of theoretical orientations could be both an opportunity for learning from each other's style or a source of much frustration and potential conflict should either the supervisor or supervisee stubbornly hold fast to their own theoretical world view. As with other issues in clinical supervision, differences of theoretical orientation are best discussed before the supervisory relationship is established. This allows for clarification of expectations, an understanding of possible challenges and benefits, and an informed decision before entering into the supervision contract.

As noted above, there can be a great opportunity for learning through differing theoretical orientations. The various perspectives, underlying assumptions, and related intervention strategies may well expand and enrich a supervisee's background and skill set. If a supervisee is looking to gain more depth in a particular theoretical orientation, then the theoretical match between supervisor and supervisee becomes most important and depth of learning will be assured.

Diversity Issues: As in the practice of psychotherapy, diversity issues also present a potential obstacle in the supervisory relationship. Differences in culture, ethnicity, religion, age, gender, and sexual orientation could undermine the relationship if not properly understood and integrated into the supervisory relationship. Borders et al. (2011) described the importance of diversity and advocacy in clinical supervision. They noted that all supervision was multicultural and advised its considerations be addressed in both the supervisor's approach to supervision and the supervisee's work with their clients. Advocacy was encouraged not just for the individual but also for the family, community, and societal influences that affect them. Of particular note in the literature was the challenge for older, White supervisors who may struggle with generational differences in training and awareness of the social power inherent in their supervisory role and the more modern socially constructed view of gender, opposing sexism and encouraging sensitivity and action toward women's issues (Inman et al., 2014). When differences in generational training and younger professionals' expectations and experiences collide, diversity concerns can become a focal point for supervisory conflict.

Diversity issues affect values, perspective, behavior, and communication styles. It is vitally important for the supervisor to have training in diversity and how to handle these issues in supervision. It is also important for the supervisee to understand how diversity may affect their relationship with their supervisor. Will their interaction be confrontational, deferential, or mutually respectful?

One way of enhancing one's skill in handling diversity is to seek continuing education in counseling and supervision with diverse populations. Another is to be prepared to engage a process of active discovery in learning and understanding of differences through the suspension of assumptions and open communication about one's experiences. Diversity can be a rich source of understanding for both the supervisor and supervisee.

An ever-increasing emphasis on multicultural and diversity training in counseling programs has heightened awareness and skill levels. It is now commonplace for supervisees and supervisors to be better informed about personal biases and prejudices (Doughty & Leddick, 2007). However gender bias of supervisees and supervisors is often overlooked. Chung, Marshall, and Gordon (2001) strongly recommended that gender bias issues be addressed within the supervisee and supervisor relationship. In their study they found that male supervisors were more likely to give a negative evaluation of female supervisees than males. Granello (2003) discovered that supervisors of both genders requested male supervisees' thoughts and opinions two times more often than female supervisees'. The opposite was true when female supervisees offered suggestions. Both male and female supervisees were more likely to use those suggestions than those offered by male supervisees. It is clear that unconscious gender bias can influence both supervisor and supervisee behavior.

To counteract these influences, it is essential that issues of diversity be addressed in the beginning of the supervisory relationship. Gatmon, Jackson, Koshkarian, and Martos-Perry (2001) conducted a study of 289 pre-doctoral psychology interns and discovered that supervisees who discussed gender issues such as similarities and differences were overall more satisfied with the quality of their supervision.

Finally, it appears that the issue of sexual orientation has not received as much attention in the counseling supervision literature (Inman et al., 2014) and is often absent from supervision discussions (Hernandez et al., 2009). Openness and comfort in addressing sexual orientation in supervision is essential to assist both lesbian, gay, bisexual, transgendered, and queer (LGBTQ) supervisees and the clients with whom they work.

Inattention to Potentially Harmful Effects of Treatment: Although it is recognized there is established research evidence that psychotherapy works, it is less recognized that there is also evidence that some clients fail to benefit and others even deteriorate while in treatment (Lambert & Ogles, 2004). Lilienfeld (2007) called for renewed attention to the potentially deleterious effects of psychotherapy as a crucial aspect of effective practice. Castonguay, Boswell, Constantino, Goldfried, and Hill (2010) detailed a working list of some 20 recommendations for minimizing these potentially harmful effects. These recommendations fell into five categories including: enhancing the therapeutic relationship, appropriate use of empirically supported treatments and techniques, prevention and repair of toxic therapy relationships and technical processes, the adjustment of treatment choice and outcome expectations due to client characteristics and type of problem, and therapist treatment for unresolved personal problems that impede their effectiveness.

It is of course vital that the supervisory relationship be strong enough to address these issues. Both supervisees and supervisors need to be aware of the potentially harmful effects of psychotherapy treatment and be ready to implement strategies for avoiding or minimizing possible harm to clients.

Failure to Utilize Outcome Data: The failure to utilize objective therapy outcome and process feedback can significantly reduce therapeutic and supervisory effectiveness. These valuable tools help assess signs of improvement or decline. Lambert (2007) found simple, session-by-session feedback can help identify and decrease rates of therapeutic deterioration. There are a number of instruments designed to do this. Two of these are the Outcome Questionnaire (Lambert, 2007) and the Treatment Outcome Package (Krause, Seligman, & Jordan, 2005). The most effective instruments should be brief, user-friendly, and acceptable to clients, supervisees, and supervisors.

Other instruments have been designed to assess the quality of the therapeutic relationship, therapist's level of engagement, client's openness to their experience and critical incidents in therapy (Greenberg & Pinsof, 1986; Hill & Lambert, 2004; Llewelyn, 1988). Effective supervision includes an assessment of client progress. This allows supervisees to become aware of their ongoing impact on clients, to better understand their strengths and weaknesses, and to alter their therapeutic approach. Objective outcome and process feedback thus improves supervisee skill and therapeutic results.

Lack of Ethical Behavior: Unethical behavior can destroy a supervisory relationship as quickly as it does a therapeutic relationship. It is the supervisor's responsibility to understand and apply the ethical guidelines for the provision of supervision as defined by their respective professional association (ACA, 2014; AMHCA, 2015; NASW, 2017; APA, 2017). It is also important for the supervisee to be informed of the ethical guidelines of clinical supervision so they may be both knowledgeable and confident about their use in supervision. Should an infraction become evident, it is necessary to provide specific feedback to the offending party, outline the ethical guideline, and request future compliance. Should these efforts fail, the next step is to file a complaint with the offending party's professional association, credentialing board, and/or state licensing agency. Ethics are meant to protect clients, supervisees, and the integrity of the profession. There is no room for unethical behavior in the supervisory relationship. However, as the scope of supervision grows, the counseling profession must also recognize the challenging legal and ethical consequences of supervisory demands and expectations (Cobia & Boes, 2000).

Formality: An overly formal supervisory style can seriously inhibit the supervisory relationship and limit supervisee clinical education. Dual supervisory roles can also inhibit effective supervision. Acting as a workplace manager and a clinical supervisor can cause role strain in trying to balance job accountability with maintenance of a facilitative supervisory alliance (Wong & Lee, 2015). Many times, a more experienced and senior professional colleague will provide supervision. This colleague will likely have status over the supervisee. This colleague may be a college professor, an employer, or a clinical director. For effective supervision to occur, these professional boundaries and the formality they often engender are best set aside to allow room for rapport, trust, and open supervisee reflection and disclosure to occur. Supervisees will likely remember the encouragement, personal support, and confidence their supervisor helped them experience, rather than the status of the supervisor's position or their expert insights into a particular case. As in psychotherapy, being respectful, genuine, and self-disclosing provides the supervisee a safe place to learn, to experiment, to succeed, and sometimes to falter on their way to becoming an even more skilled therapist.

Of course, all supervisors have the potential to become harmful (Ammirati & Kaslow, 2017). Harm can occur in many ways. Some examples include supervision that is too directive, humiliating, or punitive. If the supervisor comes from a position of authority, superiority, or judgmental evaluation, this will stifle supervisee engagement, meaningful reflection, and open disclosure. If, instead, the supervisor creates an environment of safety and models vulnerability and self-disclosure, then a collaborative and collegial relationship can emerge.

Of particular challenge to the supervisory role is healthy and effective attention to the gatekeeping role in clinical supervision. Assessment, evaluation, and feedback are important for supervisee growth and development, as well as ethical clinical practice (Bernard & Goodyear, 2014). In the academic setting there is a clear expectation of evaluation but in the work setting, that expectation often decreases with the therapeutic autonomy of the counselor. Still, mechanisms for feedback and evaluation of performance often occur in the workplace. Depending upon the professional maturity of the counselor this may involve direct observation of clinical work, individual supervision with direct supervisory input, case conference group supervision with peer feedback, and/or client feedback provided directly to the treating therapist. While no single approach may address all the needs of the gatekeeping function, in combination that may create sufficient support and ongoing assessment of counselor performance.

Discussion Questions #3:

1. As offered in this section, there are many factors influencing the supervisory relationship. Which of these will be the most difficult to discuss in this relationship?

_____

_____

_____

_____

2. Discuss the importance of dialogue and focus on diversity issues in the supervisory relationship.

_____

_____

_____

_____

Structural Factors

Time: The commitment to supervision requires setting aside both scheduled meeting time and unscheduled consultation time. Most supervision is conducted within a typical therapy hour format. Group supervision may be scheduled up to one and a half hours in length. Unscheduled consultation time may involve telephone calls, emails, or quick drop-in visits. Time can become an obstacle if the supervisor is tightly scheduled, runs late for appointments, or is unavailable outside of scheduled appointments. As with any professional obligation, it is important for the supervisor to make sure they can fulfill the needs of the supervisee or the supervisee may become frustrated and this may undermine the rapport between them. If a supervisor has agreed to supervise practicum or internship students, the supervisor must also expect to complete necessary paperwork issued by the students' academic program. The obligation to supervise another professional typically involves much more than an hour of supervision a week, so managing time is a very important supervisory skill.

Equipment: Old school supervision equipment primarily involved the use of an audiotape recorder. This was replaced with videotape. Today most training facilities utilize digital streaming technology or live observation through a two-way mirror or remote viewing via digital camera with immediate "room-to-room" telephone communication and feedback. These are the basic tools of supervision. While most supervision involves conversation between the supervisor and supervisee, use of the latest technology can greatly improve the quality and depth of supervision. This brings supervision into the "here and now." It is less likely that a supervisor will take the time to review a complete recording of a therapy session. Instead they will typically ask the supervisee to prepare in advance the parts of the recording they would like to discuss in supervision. This helps establish a focus for the supervision session and more accurately attends to the supervisee's needs. The lack of good supervision technology and equipment can greatly hinder the supervisee's experience. Despite the prevalence of state-of-the-art recording technology, research suggests that only 24 percent of supervisors observe their supervisees' clinical work on a regular basis (Amerikaner & Rose, 2012). Perhaps this is a function of limited time, professional autonomy, or supervisory presumption of supervisee skill. None the less, this may speak to the underutilization of the most basic of clinical data, observation of actual performance.

Setting: Clients seek psychotherapy in a variety of settings. Some of these include: schools, colleges, health centers, hospitals, community mental health centers, private practices, hospices, and workplaces. Each setting often directs its services to a particular type of clientele. These could include: children, college students, medical patients, adults, chronically mentally ill, the dying, and employees. This range of practice setting and clientele offers many options to the supervisee seeking a particular kind of experience. Supervisors who have a similar interest and experience with a certain setting and clientele offer more focus to the supervisee. Each setting often has different norms of practice, unique environmental challenges, and sometimes a variety of allied professionals on its treatment team. Matching the supervisee and supervisor to the setting and clientele they prefer will improve supervision effectiveness. Mismatching often results in a longer learning curve and may potentially undermine the supervisee's experience.

Facility Support: As in any office setting, supervisees will need an appropriate facility from which to conduct their work. This means a private room, furniture, appropriate office supplies and forms, telephone, a computer, and digital recording equipment. If a facility cannot provide these basic needs, then the supervisee is likely to feel like a second-class staff member and will struggle. Sometimes supervisees will share an office together or use whatever office comes available. This can work but the instability may increase anxiety and could fester into resentment. Supervisees are best treated as colleagues and provided all the necessary facility support they need, like any other professional staff member.

Staff Support: It is typically not enough for one member of a practice group to conduct clinical supervision without the support of the other group members. Everyone from the receptionist and office personnel to all of the clinical staff must be supportive. A supervisee will have many questions beyond the case material they bring for supervision. They may need to learn about scheduling, billing, access to computers, digital recording equipment, office policies, release of information protocols, and community referral resources. They may also want to "pick the brains" of many professional staff, to learn about their areas of specialization. Support from the entire facility will be necessary for the supervisee to thrive. While student supervisees, who are sure to make many mistakes, need the understanding and help of the whole staff, even professional supervisees will feel more supported if their supervisory needs are recognized by the entire staff.

Cyber-supervision: Today's proliferation of personally accessible advanced computer technology, online counseling programs, and encryption software have made the convenience and ethical use of cyber-supervision a reality. While the benefits with respect to time, travel, and convenience, as compared to face-to-face supervision are readily apparent, potential obstacles presented by cyber-supervision are not. Technology can break down. Privacy while on the computer is not necessarily guaranteed. Long-term management and destruction of clinical information, computer files, and supervision session material must be addressed. Then there are the relational aspects of the supervisor/supervisee interaction. While cyber-supervision can transmit video and audio communication, it may not as readily communicate affective, non-verbal, or sensitive temporal aspects of supervisory working alliance. How do you dialogue about sensitive information? How do you develop and maintain deeper trust that facilitates reflection and disclosure? What happens when the technology fails or is insufficient?

The research on the effectiveness of cyber-supervision as compared to face-to-face supervision suggested no real difference in the supervisee's or supervisor's perception of the working alliance (Chapman et al., 2011). To guard against potential problems with technology or possible weakness in the working alliance, telephone back-up supervisory sessions can be pre-planned, environmental privacy at home or the office can be engineered, and initial and periodic face-to-face supervision sessions could augment cyber-supervision sessions. This technology offers many advantages. With adequate pre-planning and incorporation of some face-to-face interaction, the problems with cyber-supervision can be reasonably managed.

This chapter focused on four main factors in supervision: the supervisor, supervisee, supervision relationship, and structural factors. With a better understanding of the factors of supervision, look over the inventory in Table 2.1, a Supervisory Styles Inventory (SSI) (Friedlander & Ward, 1984). Complete the inventory as a supervisee and supervisor. The results offer additional feedback to better ensure clear expectations and to reduce potential obstacles to effective supervision.

Upon review of the results of the inventory, check if your style fits the description from Friedlander and Ward (1984). Attractive supervisors are experienced by supervisees as warm, supportive, and often friendly.

Table 2.1. Supervisory Styles Inventory

	Supervisee				Supervisor			
	Not Very		Very		Not Very		Very	
1. goal-oriented	1 2 3 4		5 6 7		1 2 3 4		5 6 7	
2. perceptive	1 2 3 4		5 6 7		1 2 3 4		5 6 7	
3. concrete	1 2 3 4		5 6 7		1 2 3 4		5 6 7	
4. explicit	1 2 3 4		5 6 7		1 2 3 4		5 6 7	
5. committed	1 2 3 4		5 6 7		1 2 3 4		5 6 7	
6. affirming	1 2 3 4		5 6 7		1 2 3 4		5 6 7	
7. practical	1 2 3 4		5 6 7		1 2 3 4		5 6 7	
8. sensitive	1 2 3 4		5 6 7		1 2 3 4		5 6 7	
9. collaborative	1 2 3 4		5 6 7		1 2 3 4		5 6 7	
10. intuitive	1 2 3 4		5 6 7		1 2 3 4		5 6 7	
11. reflective	1 2 3 4		5 6 7		1 2 3 4		5 6 7	
12. responsive	1 2 3 4		5 6 7		1 2 3 4		5 6 7	
13. structured	1 2 3 4		5 6 7		1 2 3 4		5 6 7	
14. evaluative	1 2 3 4		5 6 7		1 2 3 4		5 6 7	
15. friendly	1 2 3 4		5 6 7		1 2 3 4		5 6 7	
16. flexible	1 2 3 4		5 6 7		1 2 3 4		5 6 7	
17. prescriptive	1 2 3 4		5 6 7		1 2 3 4		5 6 7	
18. didactic	1 2 3 4		5 6 7		1 2 3 4		5 6 7	
19. thorough	1 2 3 4		5 6 7		1 2 3 4		5 6 7	
20. focused	1 2 3 4		5 6 7		1 2 3 4		5 6 7	
21. creative	1 2 3 4		5 6 7		1 2 3 4		5 6 7	
22. supportive	1 2 3 4		5 6 7		1 2 3 4		5 6 7	
23. open	1 2 3 4		5 6 7		1 2 3 4		5 6 7	
24. realistic	1 2 3 4		5 6 7		1 2 3 4		5 6 7	
25. resourceful	1 2 3 4		5 6 7		1 2 3 4		5 6 7	
26. invested	1 2 3 4		5 6 7		1 2 3 4		5 6 7	
27. facilitative	1 2 3 4		5 6 7		1 2 3 4		5 6 7	
28. therapeutic	1 2 3 4		5 6 7		1 2 3 4		5 6 7	
29. positive	1 2 3 4		5 6 7		1 2 3 4		5 6 7	
30. trusting	1 2 3 4		5 6 7		1 2 3 4		5 6 7	
31. informative	1 2 3 4		5 6 7		1 2 3 4		5 6 7	
32. humorous	1 2 3 4		5 6 7		1 2 3 4		5 6 7	
33. warm	1 2 3 4		5 6 7		1 2 3 4		5 6 7	

For supervisee: Indicate your perception of the style of your current or most recent supervisor of psychotherapy/counseling on each of the following descriptors. Circle the number on the scale, from 1 to 7, that best reflects your view of him or her.

For supervisors: Indicate your perceptions of your style as a supervisor of psychotherapy/counseling on each of the following descriptors. Circle the number on the scale, from 1 to 7, that best reflects your view of yourself.

Scoring Key:
Attractive: Sum items 15, 16, 22, 23, 29, 30, 33; divide by 7.
Interpersonally sensitive: Sum items 2, 5, 10, 11, 21, 25, 26, 28; divide by 8.
Task-oriented: Sum items 1, 3, 4, 7, 13, 14, 17, 18, 19, 20; divide by 10.
Filler items: 6, 8, 9, 12, 24, 27, 31, 32.

Interpersonally sensitive supervisors are experienced as invested in the therapeutic process and what was happening to the supervisee. The task-oriented supervisor is experienced as providing structure to the supervision session and focusing on the goals and tasks of supervision (Russell-Chapin et al., 2016; Russell-Chapin & Ivey, 2004).

According to Ladany, Marotta, and Muse-Burke (2001) as supervisees gain general experience, they become more adept at case conceptualization. In their research, the SSI was administered to supervisees measuring their perceptions of their supervisors. The overall outcome of the research was that supervisees preferred supervisors who were moderately high on all three styles: attractive, interpersonally sensitive, and task-oriented (Russell-Chapin & Ivey, 2004).

Discussion Questions #4:

1. How are your responses different as a supervisor and a supervisee?

   _____

   _____

   _____

2. These distinctions and similarities may be very important as you develop your own style. What have you discovered?

   _____

   _____

   _____

Neurocounseling and Its Implication for Supervisory Obstacles

In Chapter One a general discussion of the brain lobes was observed. In the following chapters the authors use a more specific illustration of the differing brain locations and functions. Of course, the brain never functions in isolation, and a healthy brain works like a super highway accessing so many of the different brain networks. The Head Map of Function (HMF) is just one example of the unique brain sites and functions that many of the clinical supervision theories and skills utilize.

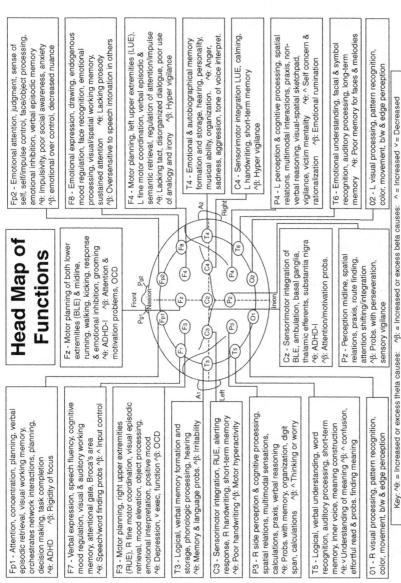

Figure 2.1 Head Map of Functions illustrates the 10–20 system of brain sites and functions.

Source: 2018 ©John S. Anderson. Permission granted by John S. Anderson

When the concept of obstacles in supervision arise though, it makes such sense to take time to solve the concerns using the entire brain, but mostly the prefrontal cortex. Look at the functions in Fp1/Fp2 and F/3 and F/4. Activating these functions will readily assist the supervisee and supervisor to resolve any needed concerns. If the problem cannot be solved, then the prefrontal cortex will certainly aid in finding necessary resources and possibly Plan B. Of course, establishing rapport and a healthy supervisory relationship has to occur before problem solving can begin.

Summary

The focus of this chapter was to understand that obstacles are a natural part of supervision, however the best way to assure effective supervision is to take ample time to assess the match between the supervisor and supervisee upfront and proactively attend to any mismatch issue that might derail the supervisory process. Supervisors should attend to all the necessary structural needs, managing time, supervision focus, facility, and staff support. All supervisors should maintain a high level of competence and actively participate in continuing education to enhance their knowledge and skills. The supervisee should be ready to engage a reflective posture, display a learning attitude, take responsibility for their part in the supervisory contract, be open to feedback, be assertive about their needs, and when necessary approach conflicts with the intention to resolve them. Finally effective supervision is best guaranteed when both the supervisor and supervisee are open to the wide array of personal and professional issues that find their way into the supervisory process. Few obstacles are impossible to overcome and can be readily managed with honesty, clear communication, a supportive and encouraging attitude, and a collegial approach. Understanding what brain functions and sites are used in overcoming obstacles assists in problem-solving behaviors as well.

Chapter Two Final Discussion Question:

Which of the supervisory factors will present the largest obstacle for you: the supervisee, supervisor, relationship, or the structural elements? Please respond in-depth with your concerns.

_____

_____

_____

_____

References

Adams, C.M., Puig, A., Baggs, A., & Pence Wolf, C. (2015). Integrating religion and spirituality into counselor education: Barriers and strategies. *Counselor Education and Supervision*, 54(1), 44–56. doi.org/10.1002/j.1556–6978.2015.00069.x

American Counseling Association (ACA) (2014). ACA code of ethics and standards of practice. Alexandria, VA: Author.

American Mental Health Counselors Association (AMHCA) (2015). Code of ethics of the American Mental Health Counselors Association. Alexandria, VA: Author.

American Psychological Association (APA) (2017). APA code of ethics and conduct. Washington, DC: Author.

Amerikaner, M. & Rose, T. (2012). Direct observation of psychology supervisees' clinical work: A snapshot of current practice. *The Clinical Supervisor*, 31, 61–80. doi:10.1080/073 25223.2012.671721f10.1080/07325223.2012.671721

Ammirati, R.J. & Kaslow, N.J. (2017). All supervisors have the potential to be harmful. *The Clinical Supervisor*, 36 (1), 116–123. doi/abs/10.1080/07325223.2017.1298071

Backlund, M. & Johnson, V. (2018). The beauty of client and supervisee resistance. *Counseling Today*, 61(2), 47–51.

Bernard, J. (1979). Supervisor training: A discrimination model. *Counselor Education and Supervision*, 19, 60–68.

Bernard, J.M. & Goodyear, R.K. (2014). *Fundamentals of clinical supervision* (5th ed.). Boston: Allyn & Bacon.

Besley, A.C. & Edwards, R. (2005). Editorial poststructuralism and the impact of the work of Michel Foucault in counselling and guidance. *Journal of Guidance & Counselling*, 33, 277–281.

Beutler, L.E., Blatt, S.J., Alimohamed, S., Levy, K.N., & Angtuaco, L. (2006). Participant factors in treating dysphoric disorders. In L.G. Castonguay & L.E. Beutoer (Eds.), *Principles of therapeutic change that work* (pp. 13–63). New York, NY: Oxford University Press.

Borders, L.D. & Giordano, A.L. (2016). Confronting confrontation in clinical supervision: An analytic autoethnography. *Journal of Counseling and Development*, 94(4), 454–463. doi:10.1002/jcad.12104

Borders, L.D., DeKruyf, L., Fernado, D.M., Fernando, H.L., Hays, D.G., Page, B., & Welfare, L.E. (2011). Best practices. Retrieved from www.acesonline.net/wp-content/uploads/2011/10/ACES-Best-practices-in-clinical-supervision-document-FINAL.pdf

Castonguay, L.G., Boswell, J.F., Constantino, M.J., Goldfried, M.R., & Hill, C.E. (2010). Training implications of harmful effects of psychological treatments. *American Psychologist*, 65(1), 34–49.

Center for Credentialing and Education (CCE) (2019). Greensboro, NC: Author.

Chapman, R.A., Baker, S.B., Nassar-McMillan, S.C., & Gerler, E.R. (2011). Cybersupervision: Further examination of synchronous and asynchronous modalities in counseling practicum supervision. *Counselor Education and Supervision*, 50, 298–313. Retrieved from http://onlinnelibrary,wiley,com/journal/10.1002/%28ISSN%291556-6978

Chung, Y.B., Marshall, J.A., & Gordon, L.L. (2001). Racial and gender biases in supervisory evaluation and feedback. *The Clinical Supervisor*, 20(1), 99–111.

Cobia, D.C. & Pipes, R.B. (2002). Mandated supervision: An intervention for disciplined professionals. *Journal of Counseling and Development*, 78, 293–296.

Cobia, D.C. & Boes, S.R. (2000). Professional disclosure statements and formal plans for supervision: Two strategies for minimizing the risk of ethical conflicts in postmaster's supervision. *Journal of Counseling and Development*, 78, 293–296.

Cooper, J.B. & Ng, K. (2009). Trait emotional intelligence and perceived supervisory working alliance of counseling trainees and their supervisors in agency settings. *International Journal for the Advancement of Counselling*, 31, 145–157. doi:10.1007/s10447-009-9074-4

Crocket, K. (2007). Counselling supervision and the production of professional selves. *British Association for Counselling and Psychotherapy*, 7(1), 19–25.

Doughty, E.A. & Leddick, G.R. (2007). Gender differences in the supervisory relationship. *Journal of Professional Counseling: Practice, Theory, and Research*, 35(2), 17–30.

Downs, L. (2000). A literature review of gender issues in supervision: Power differentials and dual relationship. (ERIC Document Reproduction Service No. ED444077)

Falender, C.A. & Shafranske, E.P. (2004). *Clinical supervision: A competency-based approach*. Washington, DC: American Psychological Association.

Fall, M. & Sutton, J. (2004). *Clinical supervision: A handbook for practitioners*. Boston: Pearson Allyn & Bacon.

Feltham, C. (2000). Counselling supervision: Baselines, problems, and possibilities. In B.L. Lawton & C. Feltham (Eds.), *Taking supervision forward: Enquiries and trends in counseling and psychotherapy* (pp. 5–24). London: Sage.

Friedlander, M.L. & Ward, L.G. (1984). Development and validation of the Supervisory Styles Inventory. *Journal of Counseling Psychology*, 31, 541–557.

Gatmon, D., Jackson, D., Koshkarian, L., & Martos-Perry, N. (2001). Exploring ethnic, gender and sexual orientation variables in supervision: Do they really matter? *Journal of Multicultural Counseling and Development*, 29, 102–114.

Granello, D.H. (2003). Influence strategies in the supervisory dyad: An investigation into the effects of gender and age. *Counselor Education and Supervision*, 42, 189–202.

Greenberg, L.S. & Pinsof, W.M. (Eds.). (1986). *The psychotherapeutic process: A research handbook*. New York, NY: Guilford Press.

Greenson, R.R. (1967). *The technique and practice of psychoanalysis* (Vol. 1). New York, NY: International University Press.

Henry, W.P., Strupp, H.H., Butler, S.F., Schacht, T.E., & Binder, J.L. (1993). The effects of training in time-limited dynamic psychotherapy: Changes in therapeutic behavior. *Journal of Consulting and Clinical Psychology*, 61, 434–440.

Hernandez, P., Taylor, B., & McDowell, T. (2009). Listening to ethnic minority AAMFT approved supervisors: Reflections on their experiences as supervisors. *Journal of Systemic Therapies*, 28, 88–100. doi:10.1521/jsyt.2009.28.1.88

Hill, C.E. & Lambert, M.J. (2004). Methodological issues in studying psychotherapy process and outcomes. In M.J. Lambert (Ed.), Bergin and Garfield's *Handbook of psychotherapy and behavior change* (5th ed., pp. 84–135). New York, NY: Wiley.

Hill, H.R., Crowe, T.P., & Gonsalvez, C.J. (2015). Reflective dialogue in clinical supervision: A pilot study involving collaborative review of supervision videos. *Psychotherapy Research*, 26(3), 263–278. doi.org/10.1080/10503307.214.996795

Holloway, E.L. (1995). *Clinical supervision: A systems approach*. Thousand Oaks, CA: Sage.

Inman, A.G., Hutman, H., Pendse, A., Devdas, L., Luu, L., & Ellis, M.V. (2014). Current trends concerning supervisors, supervisees, and clients in clinical supervision. In C.E. Watkins, Jr. & D. Milne (Eds.), *Wiley international handbook of clinical supervision* (pp. 61–102). Oxford: Wiley.

Kraus, D.R., Seligman, D.A., & Jordan, J.R. (2005). Validation of a behavioral health treatment outcome and assessment tool designed for naturalistic settings: The treatment outcome package. *Journal of Clinical Psychology*, 61, 285–314.

Ladany, N., Marotta, S., & Muse-Burke, J.L. (2001). Counselor experience related to complexity of case conceptualization and supervision preference. *Counselor Education and Supervision*, 40, 203–219.

Lambert, M.J. (2007). Presidential address: What we have learned from a decade of research aimed at improving outcome in routine care. *Psychotherapy Research*, 17, 1–14.

Lambert, M.J. & Ogles, B.M. (2004). The efficacy and effectiveness of psychotherapy. In M.J. Lambert (Ed.), Bergin and Garfield's *Handbook of psychotherapy and behavioral change* (5th ed., pp. 139–193). New York, NY: Wiley.

Lenz, A.S., Sangganjanavanich, V.F., Balkin, R.S., Oliver, M., & Smith, R.L. (2012). Wellness model of supervision: A comparative analysis. *Counselor Education and Supervision*, 51, 207–221. doi:10.1002/j.1556–6978.2012.00015.x

Lilienfeld, S.O. (2007). Psychological treatments that cause harm. *Perspectives on Psychological Science*, 2, 53–70.

Llewelyn, S.P. (1988). Psychological therapy as viewed by clients and therapists. *British Journal of Clinical Psychology*, 27, 223–237.

McMurtery, R.F., Webb, T.T., & Arnold, R.D. (2011). Assessing perceptions and attitudes of intimate behavior in clinical supervision among licensed professional counselors, licensed social workers, and licensed psychologists. *The Researcher: An Interdisciplinary Journal*, 24(2), 57–78. Retrieved from http://connectoin.ebscohost.com/c/articles/67298447/assessing-perceptions-attitides-intimate-behaviors-clinical-supvision-among-licensed-professional-counselors-licensed-social-workers-licensed-psychologists

Meany-Walen, K.K., Davis-Gage, D., & Lindo, N.A. (2016). The impact of wellness-focused supervision on mental health counseling practicum students. *Journal of Counseling and Development*, 94(4), 464–472. doi.org/10.1002/jcad.12105

Merriman, J. (2015). Enhancing counselor supervision through compassion fatigue education. *Journal of Counseling and Development*, 93(3), 370–378. doi.org/10.1002/jcad.12035

Morgan, M.M. & Sprenkle, D.H. (2007). Toward a common-factor approach to supervision. *Journal of Marital and Family Therapy*, 33(1), 1–17.

National Association of Social Workers (NASW) (2017). Code of ethics. Washington, DC: NASW Press.

Nelson, M.L., Barnes, K.L., Evans, A.L., & Triggiano, P.J. (2008). Working with conflict in clinical supervision: Wise supervisors' perspectives. *Journal of Counseling Psychology*, 55, 172–184. doi:10.1037/0022-0167.55.2.172

Prouty, A. (2001). Experiencing feminist family therapy supervision. *Journal of Feminist Family Therapy*, 12, 171–203.

Rapisarda, C.A., Desmind, K.J., & Nelson, J.R. (2011). Student reflections on the journey to being a supervisor. *The Clinical Supervisor*, 30, 109–123. doi:10.1080/07325223.2011.564958

Rapisarda, C.A. & Britton, P.J. (2007). Sanctioned supervision: Voices from the experts. *Journal of Mental Health Counseling*, 29(1), 81–92.

Reese, R.J., Toland, M.D., & Slone, N.C. (2010). Effect of client feedback on couple psychotherapy outcomes. *Psychotherapy Theory, Research, Practice Training*, 47 (4), 616–630.

Ronnestad, M.H. & Skovholt, T.M. (2003). The journey of the counselor and therapist: Research findings and perspectives on professional development. *Journal of Career Development*, 30, 5–44.

Russell-Chapin, L.A. (2007). Supervision: An essential for professional counselor development. In J. Gregoire & C.M. Jungers (Eds.), *The counselor's companion: What every beginning counselor needs to know* (pp. 79–88). Mahwah, NJ: Lawrence Erlbaum.

Russell-Chapin, L.A., Sherman, N.E., & Ivey, A.E. (2016). *Your supervised practicum and internship: Field resources for turning theory into action* (2nd ed.). New York, NY: Routledge.

Russell-Chapin, L.A. & Ivey, A.E. (2004). *Your supervised practicum and internship: Field resources for turning theory into action.* Pacific Grove, CA: Brooks/Cole.

Strupp, H.H. & Hadley, S.W. (1985). Negative effects and their determinants. In D.T. Mays & C.M. Franks (Eds.), *Negative outcome in psychotherapy and what to do about it* (pp. 20–55). New York, NY: Springer.

Thomas, J.T. (2005). Licensing board complaints: Minimizing the impact on the psychologist's defense and clinical practice. *Professional Psychology: Research and Practice*, 36, 426–433.

West, W. & Clark, V. (2004). Learning from a qualitative study into counseling supervision: Listening to supervisor and supervisee. *Counselling and Psychotherapy Research*, 4(2), 20–26.

Wolberg, L.R. (1967). *The technique of psychotherapy* (2nd ed.). New York, NY: Grune & Stratton.

Wong, P.Y. & Lee, A.E. (2015). Dual roles of social work supervisors: Strain and strengths as managers and clinical supervisors. *China Journal of Social Work*, 8(2), 164–181. doi/abs/10.1080/17525098.2015.1039168

3
ETHICS IN COUNSELING SUPERVISION

Overview

In many respects, there is no more important relationship in the evolution of a developing professional counselor than that of clinical supervisor and supervisee. The clinical supervisor is at the same time a coach, mentor, teacher, evaluator, and role model. Through this complex relationship the foundation for the counselor's professional values and ethical behavior is formed.

The ethical framework surrounding the supervisor/supervisee relationship provides critically important guidelines for the establishment of a meaningful and respectful professional partnership. By maintaining appropriate boundaries, applying a sound theoretically established supervisory process, and providing essential feedback in a fair, accurate, honest, and respectful manner, the ethical supervisor can be best assured of preparing the supervisee for a successful future as a skilled mental health practitioner (Russell-Chapin, Sherman & Ivey, 2016; Russell-Chapin & Ivey, 2004).

This chapter will focus on the ethical practice of clinical supervision. Each section will present an ethical problem that could readily arise in any setting where mental health services are provided. The reader will be presented the problem and a set of discussion questions intended to encourage further reflection on the particular ethical issues involved in that situation. Then a short summary of the relevant ethical guidelines will be provided followed by a suggested course of appropriate action. For purposes of this discussion, the ethical Guidelines of the American Counseling Association (ACA) will be employed to both guide the authors' analysis of the ethical problem and to help outline an ethically appropriate course of action. Please note, readers are encouraged to review their own specific professional association's ethical guidelines as they relate to the ethical delivery of clinical supervision. While the reader will likely find much consistency and overlap, your association's guidelines will be those employed should you need to defend your action in front of a disciplinary review committee, whether that be the American Psychological Association (2017), National Association of Social Workers (2017), American Mental Health Counselors Association (2015), or any other professional association and division in which you are a member such as the American Counseling Association (2014).

Many of the above codes and others may be viewed online through the associations' homepages. Frequently used web addresses are listed at the end of this chapter in Appendix 3.A. In addition there is a supplemental booklet available through this publisher entitled *Codes of Ethics for the Helping Professions* with codes from all helping professions such as the American Psychological Association, the National Association of Social Workers, and the National Organization for Human Service Education. This booklet is available to purchase.

Finally, the chapter will end with a brief discussion of the function of disciplinary review and typical disciplinary consequences of unethical behavior.

Goals

- Define and identify possible ethical dilemmas and behaviors.
- Locate resources for resolutions of ethical concerns.
- Understand how counseling supervision ethics frame the supervision relationship.

Ethical Supervision Behaviors and Standards of Care

When one goes to any professional as a consumer of services, there is a certain expectation of professional standard of care. Russell-Chapin and

Ivey (2004) state, "You expect your chosen expert to have expertise and knowledge in the services you desire. You expect to be treated respectfully and competently" (p. 162). This holds true in the clinical supervision world as well.

Ethical behaviors are typically guided by written organizational mandates adopted by a specific discipline. Ethical codes are designed to, of course, protect the consumer, but appropriate ethical codes also protect the supervisor and the profession. These documents were written by members of that particular professional organization to assist in providing quality treatment to the client and always doing no harm (Baird, 2002).

For example the Association for Counselor Education and Supervision (ACES) ethical guidelines for counseling supervisors address client welfare and rights, program administration role, and supervisory role. These three components all have ethical aspects. Understanding that clinical supervision ethics and ethical behaviors must be the underpinnings of competent supervision is essential. These ethical guidelines were incorporated into the ACA ethical guidelines in 2005. The current ACA Guidelines include ethics for supervisors (2014).

As stated earlier in Chapter One, supervisees and supervisors must articulate the expectations, rules, and boundaries in the supervisory relationship. This begins with a signed Informed Consent that delineates responsibilities and logistics (Williamson & Williamson, 2018).

Corey, Corey, and Callanan (2003) outlined procedural steps to assist supervisees in addressing ethical concerns: identify the problem or dilemma; identify potential issues involved; review relevant codes, know applicable laws and regulations; obtain consultation; consider possible courses of action; look at the consequences of various decisions; and finally decide the best course of action. The authors are not suggesting that these steps must be linear, but the model may be an excellent, beginning method to use in a supervisory session to begin to resolve any ethical issues (Haynes, Corey, & Moulton, 2003). As the ethical dilemmas are presented in the following pages, use the steps outlined above to assist in the reflection anecdotes and resolution of the ethical concerns.

Discussion Question #1:

As you read the procedural steps for addressing ethical concerns, identify which step will be the most difficult for you.

_____

_____

_____

_____

Client Worsens While Under the Care of Supervisee

A 16-year-old girl who came to counseling for help with recurrent depression is exhibiting increasingly severe episodes of self-mutilation. The supervisee is very worried and afraid to tell his supervisor about the extent of her self-injury for fear that it will result in a poor evaluation. Eight sessions of counseling have been completed. The client has made vague references to childhood sexual abuse but to date nothing specific has been addressed in therapy. The supervisee is reluctant to discuss the matter with his client because he is afraid she will become suicidal. The supervisee has not told his supervisor the self-mutilation has worsened.

Discussion Questions #2:

1. Should the supervisee keep this information from his supervisor?

_____

_____

_____

_____

2. Is this client at risk for suicide?

_____

_____

_____

_____

3. Is this case beyond the expertise of the supervisee?

_____

_____

_____

_____

4. What might be causing the supervisee's lack of disclosure?

_____

_____

_____

_____

5. How can the supervisor monitor the client's welfare?

_____

_____

_____

_____

The 2014 American Counseling Association (ACA) ethical guideline that applies to this problem is F.1.a. Client Welfare that states:

> A primary obligation of counseling supervisors is to monitor the services provided by other counselors or counselors-in-training. Counseling supervisors monitor client welfare and supervise clinical performance and professional development.

Possible means available to the supervisor to monitor the services provided by the supervisee are: regular meetings with the supervisee, review of client case notes, review of samples of clinical work, and/or live observations of the supervisee's therapy, and regular written evaluations whether in formal or informal formats.

In this case it is clear the supervisee is struggling but unable or unwilling to disclose their worry to their supervisor. This is not an uncommon supervisee anxiety. While there may be many problems with supervisee inadequacy and supervisor/supervisee trust, the primary ethical problem for the supervisor is, he does not know that the client is intensifying her self-mutilation. Regular supervision meetings, review of the case record, and videotaped observations of the therapy would likely have brought the matter to the supervisor's attention, where it could be appropriately evaluated and addressed with the supervisee. There are many possible remedies to this case. Perhaps the self-mutilation is increasing due to avoidance of the discussion of her abuse. Perhaps the client is not suicidal but the supervisee is confusing self-mutilation with suicidal behavior and needs some help making a differential risk assessment. Perhaps therapeutic interventions could be discussed to explore the abuse or to limit the client's self-mutilation. Or maybe, this case is too overwhelming for this supervisee at this time and a referral to another counselor is warranted, so that the client's self-harm can be more effectively managed.

Worthen and Lambert (2007) agree that it is time for supervisors to incorporate real-time feedback on client progress, outcome monitoring, and brief client assessments into regular, ongoing supervision. These authors believe it is essential to build in a supervisory outcome management system to ensure that client's and supervisee's goals are maximized. In a research project, Hannan, Lambert, Harmon, Nielsen, Smart, and Shimokawa (2005) asked 48 therapists, 22 were licensed and 26 were trainees, to rate their 550 clients of a three-week period on client progress and client deterioration. These counselors knew that there was a statistical base rate of 8 percent of client deterioration. Even with that information, rarely were they able to predict a negative outcome. Many of the professional therapists were also supervisors. None of the supervisors correctly predicted a negative outcome. The counselors identified one out of 40 clients who deteriorated, whereas the computer statistical algorithms identified 77 percent of deteriorated clients.

This subjective optimism may assist us with difficult clients, but it does not do justice and may inhibit therapy progress with high-risk clients (Worthen & Lambert, 2007). Garb (2005) also writes that many clinicians prefer their intuitive, subjective impressions to actual statistical data and information. Moving to a more multi-perspective system of offering feedback and tracking progress is needed in our clinical supervision world.

Angry Client Wants to End Counseling with Supervisee

A 42-year-old male client is seeking counseling for help with his struggling marriage. He has had repeated affairs but states his interest in wanting to cease his infidelity and recommit to his marriage. He is very nervous about the privacy of his disclosures but is reassured by the supervisee that all of his disclosures are confidential and will not be released to anyone without his written consent. A few weeks into therapy the client becomes very angry after the supervisee told him he had been talking with his supervisor, Dr. Ellen Smith, about the case and had a good idea how to help him. Unknown to the supervisee, Dr. Ellen Smith was a good friend of the client's wife. The client now realizing that his counselor's supervisor was Dr. Ellen Smith became very angry and afraid that all he had disclosed would find its way back to his wife. He wanted to immediately end therapy with the supervisee.

Discussion Questions #3:

1. Did the supervisee sufficiently disclose the limits of confidentiality?

_____

_____

_____

_____

2. Does the client have a right to be angry with the counselor?

_____

_____

_____

_____

3. Is there a risk that this counselor could be sued and/or a complaint brought against the counselor, supervisor, and agency?

_____

_____

_____

_____

4. How can the counselor and supervisor best handle this situation?

_____

_____

_____

_____

5. What supervisee and supervisor actions could have prevented this problem?

_____

_____

_____

_____

The ACA (2014) ethical guideline that applies to this problem is F.1.c. Informed Consent and Client Rights:

> Supervisors make supervisees aware of the client rights including the protection of client privacy and confidentiality in the counseling relationship. Supervisees provide clients with professional disclosure information and inform them of how the supervision process influences the limits of confidentiality. Supervisees make clients aware of who will have access to records of the counseling relationship and how these records will be used.

The primary mistake made by this supervisee and supervisor is that the client was not "fully" informed as to "specifically" who would see the counseling records. If this had happened, the client may have immediately voiced his concern about the supervisor being a friend of his wife and his worry that his disclosures might find their way back to his wife. This could have enabled the supervisee to address the issues of confidentiality and explain that its protection also extends to his supervisor. Should the client have persisted in his objection, a referral to another therapist with a different supervisor could have been offered. In an article by Kaplan (2003), the author discussed that 80 percent or more of all ethical concerns revolve around the single issue of informed consent. To ensure that clients and supervisees understand all rights, verbal and written consent is essential.

However, in this ethical dilemma the damage had already been done. The client already made what he now perceives as potentially incriminating disclosures. The risk for a lawsuit and/or a disciplinary complaint is high. The supervisee in this situation may be best advised to make a genuine apology for their lack of full informed consent and disclosure of who will have access to the counseling records. The supervisor may also be well advised to offer a similar apology and reassurance to the client that his disclosures are confidential and will not be shared with his wife. This may in itself sufficiently reduce the client's anger and worry. If not, the client's anger and mistrust will likely undermine the therapeutic relationship and a referral to another therapist may be in order.

While not a factor in the present case, another related issue with regard to informed consent and client rights is disclosure of the supervisee's qualifications and status as a trainee. Many counselors in training are sensitive to client's perception of their professional competency. While it may be tempting to avoid this issue with clients, it is the client's right to be aware of their counselor's qualifications and to make an informed decision about who they want to help them with their concerns. In most cases, clients are more than satisfied working with a counselor in training, finding comfort in the knowledge they are being supervised by an experienced and qualified professional. In those cases where a client does object to a counselor in training, their wishes must be respected, and a referral to a fully qualified professional is appropriate.

Pressure from the Agency to Supervise the New Counseling Intern

A highly skilled, experienced, and licensed professional counselor has been asked by his agency to supervise the new counseling intern from the local University counseling program. None of the other senior agency clinicians are interested in taking on this responsibility but don't want to lose the opportunity afforded them in having the intern help them with the agency's waiting list. The agency director makes a personal appeal to a junior staff person to take on this obligation. Although reluctant and unsure how to provide adequate supervision, the junior staff person accepts the request and agrees to supervise the intern. The two meet on a regular basis, review ongoing cases, clear the agency's waiting list, and generally fulfill the intern's academic requirements.

Discussion Questions #4:

1. Is it appropriate for interns to be used to clear an agency's waiting list?

_____

_____

_____

_____

2. Does the junior staff person have sufficient experience to supervise the intern?

_____

_____

_____

_____

3. Will the intern receive a "good" experience at this agency?

_____

_____

_____

_____

4. Will the clients seen by this intern receive "good" therapy?

_____

_____

_____

_____

5. What special qualifications and training does the junior staff person have to provide the intern with a "good" supervised experience?

_____

_____

_____

_____

The ACA (2014) ethical guideline that applies to this problem is F.2.a. Counselor Supervision Competence:

> Prior to offering clinical supervision services, counselors are trained in supervision methods and techniques. Counselors who offer clinical supervision regularly pursue continuing education activities including both counseling and supervision topics and skills.

Both the NASW (2017) and APA (2017) ethical standards are also clear on this matter. Working outside of a helping professional's area of expertise may harm clients, supervisees, and the profession.

In the above situation, the junior staff member is likely a well-trained, adequately experienced, and appropriately credentialed counseling professional, but she openly acknowledged reluctance and uncertainty in providing clinical supervision of the intern. In all likelihood, the supervision she provided was adequate, the counseling the clients received was adequate, and the intern had an adequate clinical experience at this agency. However, how might the intern's experience have been enhanced if his supervisor was trained in current supervision methods and techniques? How much better could the intern's clients' therapeutic results have been? And how might the intern's overall clinical experience at this agency have been improved if they were supervised by a specially trained clinical supervisor? The answer is self-evident. All would have benefited from a far better experience, if the foundation of that experience were based upon current standards of competent clinical supervision. Polanski (2000) encourages teaching supervision at both the master's and doctoral levels. Courses at the master's level will help trainees to better understand what they need and want out of supervision and assist them in becoming better supervisors at a later developmental stage.

In this situation one might argue that some benefit is better than no benefit at all, after all, waiting-list clients were seen and the intern gained some valuable experience and met his academic requirements, but this is a proverbial "slippery slope." Today's ethical standards require that we provide competent clinical supervision. It might have been more appropriate for the agency to turn down the opportunity for the internship and, instead, send the junior agency staff member to continuing education on clinical supervision. Or perhaps the junior staff member could have sought supervision on the provision of clinical supervision from an appropriately trained University faculty member, while jointly supervising the intern at their agency. Sometimes real work demands pressure counselors into situations with which they are uncomfortable. Rather than succumbing to the demand, it is better to explore your reluctance and take proactive steps at addressing your limited qualifications. Cobia and Boes (2000) go even farther by stating that it is the supervisor's responsibility to locate another supervisor who is clinically competent in supervision.

Another issue not addressed in the above situation is competency with multicultural and diversity issues in supervision. Counselors must be aware of and sensitive to the influences of gender, ethnicity, culture, and race in supervisory relationships. As we all likely learned in our basic counseling training, individual differences, left misunderstood or misinterpreted, can easily undermine rapport, and sidetrack our most well-intended efforts. The same applies to clinical supervision. We all bring our personal biases, limited experiences, and stereotypes into every relationship we have. It is incumbent upon each of us to become aware of our limits of perception and to learn how to skillfully and respectfully address these issues as they also inevitably emerge in our supervisory relationships. Kwan (2001) reiterates this philosophy by emphasizing the importance of the counselor knowing his/herself well. Then and only then will the counselor/supervisor be ready to assist in the supervisee's development.

Using the Multicultural Competency Standards developed by Sue, Arredondo, and McDavis (1992), Kwan (2001) developed the following guidelines to assist helping professionals in exploring personal multi-cultural journeys. Although this was developed for counselors in training, the same format can be applied to supervisors in training. Read through each sentence and first decide whether as the reader there is personal agreement or disagreement with the guideline. Then reflect on the guideline's meaning. If the guideline is true or useful, then begin to dissect how it might play a role in your work with clients and supervisees.

Attitudes and Beliefs Guidelines

#1 Culturally skilled counselors believe that cultural self-awareness and sensitivity to one's own cultural heritage is essential.

#2 Culturally skilled counselors are aware of how their own cultural background and experiences have influenced attitudes, values, and biases about psychological processes.

#3 Culturally skilled counselors are able to recognize the limits of their multicultural competency and expertise.

Every human being has a culture all to him/herself. It impacts who we are and how life is experienced and handled. This, too, will definitely impact how we present ourselves in supervision as a supervisee and supervisor.

Discussion Question #5:

How will working with diverse client populations be a challenge for you as a counselor, supervisee, and supervisor?

_____

_____

_____

_____

A Close Friend and Colleague Wants You to Supervise Them

A highly trained and well-respected clinical supervisor, with years of supervisory experience, who has helped many students and professionals fulfill their clinical supervision requirements for their respective professional certification and licensure, has been asked by his friend and colleague to supervise him. It seems that the colleague's graduate counseling education program has now required all faculty to become licensed and this will require two years of clinical supervision. The supervisor, not wanting to disappoint his friend and confident he can help him, agrees to conduct the supervision. All goes well at first, but as the supervision continues, the supervisor becomes aware of some significant weaknesses in his colleague's approach. He attempts to address these directly with him, but his friend becomes defensive. The supervisor decides to back off. He does not want to hurt their relationship but the weaknesses become more obvious. The supervisor feels a professional obligation to address it again and attempts to do so. This time his friend becomes angry and demands to terminate supervision. The supervisor, now frustrated and disappointed, agrees that termination may be the best solution. For months thereafter, despite continued efforts by the supervisor to reconnect with his friend, his friend keeps his distance. The supervisor fears the relationship may be forever damaged and remains concerned that his friend has not addressed his weaknesses.

Discussion Questions #6:

1. Is it appropriate for a friend and colleague to request supervision from a friend and colleague?

   _____

   _____

   _____

   _____

2. How should the supervisor have responded to the request?

   _____

   _____

   _____

   _____

3. How could the supervisor best deliver the feedback to his friend?

_____

_____

_____

_____

4. Is termination of the supervisory relationship an appropriate option?

_____

_____

_____

_____

5. What should the supervisor do with his disappointment and continued concern?

_____

_____

_____

_____

The ACA (2014) ethical guidelines that best address this problem are F.3.a. Relationship Boundaries with Supervisees, F.3.d. and Close Relatives and Friends:

> Counseling supervisors avoid nonprofessional relationships with current supervisees. If supervisors must assume other professional roles (e.g., clinical and administrative supervisor, instructor) with supervisee, they work to minimize potential conflicts and explain to the supervisee the expectations and responsibilities associated with each role. They do not engage in any form of nonprofessional interaction that may compromise the supervisory relationship. Counseling supervisors avoid accepting close relatives, romantic partners, or friends as supervisees.

The problem above describes a difficult predicament involving collegial loyalty, friendship, and the role of the clinical supervisor. At the outset, all parties seemed satisfied with the arrangement. Although we are not clear whether the supervisor explained to the supervisee the potential conflicts, conflicting roles, and varying expectations across these roles, perhaps such a discussion might have led them to conclude that the arrangement was ill-advised. Having engaged the supervisor/supervisee relationship, they soon ran into trouble. Their friendship became tested when the supervisee rejected supervisory feedback. The eventual consequence was loss of both their friendship and supervisory relationship. The ethical guidelines clearly state that supervisory relationships with friends should be avoided. The problem involves the difficulty of managing dual relationships and their tendency to undermine one another. While some dual relationships may be unavoidable, such as administrative supervisor/colleague and supervisor/instructor, others like supervisor and friend are avoidable. Although not an issue in the above example, the ethical guidelines also prohibit sexual relationships between supervisor and supervisee and sexual harassment of supervisees.

Haynes et al. (2003, p. 171) offer several additional questions to help in determining the healthiest decision and resolution of multiple relationship issues.

- Can I explain and justify my decisions regarding supervisees to an ethics board?
- What advice would I give to a colleague who came to me with a similar situation?
- Am I willing for my actions to be public?

A Supervisee's Parent Unexpectedly Dies

A supervisor and supervisee have been meeting for supervision for well over nine months. During that time the supervisee shared that her mother was ill with cancer. It had been a difficult ordeal for her and a frequent topic in her supervision. The supervisee worked with two clients who were dealing with loss issues and it was important for her to understand how her own issues were influencing her therapy. Then the personal news came. Her mother had died. The supervisee was very upset and in tears as she informed her supervisor of the news. During their conversation she asked her supervisor to help her get through the visitation and funeral. The supervisor politely said she could not do so as it would be a breach of supervision ethics for her to have a nonprofessional relationship with her supervisee. The supervisor offered her condolences and scheduled the next supervision session.

Discussion Questions #7:

1. Was the topic of her mother's struggle with cancer appropriate content for supervision?

2. Should the supervisee continue to see clients who were also dealing with loss?

3. Did the supervisor act ethically in declining the supervisee's request to help her get through the visitation and funeral?

4. How else could the supervisor have addressed the supervisee's request?

5. What personal feelings might the supervisor be reacting to in declining the supervisee's request?

_____

_____

_____

_____

The ACA (2014) ethical guideline that applies to this situation is F.3.e Potentially Beneficial Relationships:

> Counseling supervisors are aware of the power differential in their relationships with supervisees. If they believe a nonprofessional relationship with a supervisee may be potentially beneficial to the supervisee, they take precautions similar to counselors working with clients. Examples of potentially beneficial interactions or relationships include attending a formal ceremony, hospital visits, providing support in a stressful event, or mutual membership in a professional association, organization, or community.

The supervisor in the above situation was generally acting within their appropriate boundary in citing the ethical guideline prohibiting nonprofessional relationships with supervisees, however she failed to consider the potentially beneficial relationship she could have established by helping her supervisee get through the visitation and funeral. It seems clear the issue of the supervisee's mother's struggle with cancer had been a frequent topic of their supervision. It is very likely the supervisee found support in the supervisor's therapeutic encouragement while she continued her work with clients who were dealing with their own losses. It may have been very disappointing and potentially damaging to their supervisory relationship for the supervisor to decline the supervisee's request. How will this affect their rapport and the supervisee's sense of trust and future comfort with personal disclosure? It could inhibit it. Perhaps the supervisor had strong personal reasons for declining the request. Maybe she was very uncomfortable with visitations and funerals. Maybe she felt she could not lend much effective support to her supervisee. If these were her feelings, it might have been better for her to have shared them with her supervisee and offer some other means of support. As supervisors we are not immune from our own issues and are a powerful role model to our supervisees. In discussing the matter further, the supervisor might have demonstrated how to acknowledge and work through personal shortcomings. Attending the visitation and funeral could have provided an ethically beneficial relationship to the supervisee, but not so if the supervisor lacked the confidence or ability to handle it herself.

This ethical dilemma has many unique facets. One issue that is not often addressed is the need for the supervisor to seek counseling and/or ongoing supervision. The importance of supervisors not being counselors at the same time to their supervisees is well documented. There is a fine line to be observed, however. Supervisors have the responsibility in the supervisory process to deal with supervisee's limitations, strengths, and liabilities. There could also be countertransference issues, so those, too, must be acknowledged in supervision. Much like self-disclosure in counseling, discussing supervisor's personal issues in an appropriate and relevant manner will not necessarily affect the supervisor/supervisee relationship (Sumeral & Borders, 1996). The authors of this textbook often tell supervisees this rule, "If your self-disclosure feels too good, then you know you have shared too much!" That is when the supervisor needs to seek out counseling and/or supervision.

Supervisee On-the-Job Training

A new practicum student just received his placement site notice. He is very excited about the prospect of working at one of the leading private practices in town. His initial interview went very well. The staff at the private practice offered him the position. The first day on the job he had four clients to see. He dove right in, did his case notes, and submitted the payment for the sessions to the appropriate office staff. Then his troubles began. He was told he didn't have the clients fill out the correct forms. He didn't properly schedule the next appointments. He failed to collect the right co-pays and deductibles. And worst of all, he didn't inform his clients he was a practicum student and didn't have his clients sign the appropriate release forms, so a senior staff therapist could supervise his work with them. His first day on the job was a disaster.

Discussion Questions #8:

1. Who's responsible for these problems, the supervisee or supervisor?

2. What kind of consequence should the supervisee receive?

3. How can the problem be remedied?

4. What if a client now objects to seeing a practicum student?

5. What else does the supervisee need to know?

The ACA (2014) ethical guidelines that apply to this situation include: F.4.a. Informed Consent for Supervision, F.4.b. Emergencies and Absences, and F.4.c. Standards for Supervisees:

Supervisors are responsible for incorporating into their supervision the principles of informed consent and participation. Supervisors inform supervisees of the policies and procedures to which they are expected to adhere and the mechanisms for due process appeal of individual supervisory actions. Supervisors establish and communicate to supervisees, procedures for contacting them or, in their absence, alternative on-call supervision to assist in handling crises. Supervisors make their supervisees aware of professional and ethical standards and legal responsibilities.

In the above example, the new practicum student was given no direction. He had no job orientation, no supervisory orientation, and no briefing on ethical standards and legal responsibilities. He made many mistakes. While it would have been useful for him to have asked some questions before he agreed to see clients, it would have been better yet, if he had had a few hours of practicum orientation. Many graduate programs offer this to students before they are placed in the community, but each placement site is so unique, it should provide its own orientation, complete with an initial supervisory session where expectations, procedures, policies, and appeal mechanisms can be defined. As a consequence of not having this orientation, the new practicum student, the private practice staff, and his supervisor have a mess to clean up. In addition, there is the problem of the uninformed clients who did not realize they were working with a practicum student and didn't understand the supervisory requirements associated with that relationship. Each of them need to be fully informed and offered the opportunity to either continue working with the practicum student or select a new therapist. Each of the problems created by on-the-job training can be repaired, but all of them could have been prevented if the supervisory, graduate school, and placement site responsibilities had been more fully met.

Off on the Wrong Foot and Only Getting Worse

An independent practicing master's level therapist decided she could benefit from ongoing clinical supervision. She developed a list of area practitioners who she felt she could work well with and began the process of interviewing each of them. She hoped to find a female, highly experienced clinician with Jungian training. However, after speaking with several prospective supervisors, she couldn't find exactly what she wanted. After some reflection, she decided to contract with a male supervisor who had a psychodynamic orientation. He said he was familiar with Jungian principles and more importantly had provided clinical supervision for over ten years. Their first supervision session was scheduled for two weeks later. The supervisee arrived on time but had to wait 20 minutes before her supervisor finished his last client. The session opened with the supervisor talking about himself, his experience, and his last counseling session. By the time he finished, the hour was over and the supervisee was not able to share anything about her needs and expectations, nor was she able to present a case for feedback. The counselor left the first session worried she had made a mistake in selecting this supervisor but decided to give him another try. As with the previous session, the supervisor was again late. This time he did ask her if she had a case to present and she offered a concise client history, diagnostic impression, and questions for supervision. The supervisor listened attentively and then offered his analysis from a psychodynamic, object-relations perspective. The supervisee responded with a puzzled look on her face. She asked, "What symbolism do you think might be represented in the client's dream about an old, gray-haired woman?" The supervisor shrugged his shoulders and asked the supervisee questions about the client's attachment to his mother. The supervisee said nothing. The supervisor then began to postulate about the possible implications of the client's early attachment on his current problems with anxiety. The supervisee respectfully listened but thought, "I've made a terrible mistake in choosing this supervisor. Now what do I do?" Out of courtesy and perhaps avoidance, she agreed to schedule another supervision session, but didn't show up. Instead she wrote the supervisor a letter stating her decision to discontinue their supervision. She explained she really preferred a female supervisor and thanked him for his time.

Discussion Questions #9:

1. How specific should a supervisee be in their selection of a supervisor?

_____

_____

_____

_____

2. What is the supervisor's responsibility in assuring a good supervisee/
   supervisor match?

   _____

   _____

   _____

   _____

3. If problems occur how should they be addressed?

   _____

   _____

   _____

   _____

4. Did the supervisor have a fair opportunity to adjust his approach?

   _____

   _____

   _____

   _____

5. Should the supervisee have terminated supervision in the manner
   she did?

   _____

   _____

   _____

   _____

The ACA (2014) ethical guideline that is relevant to this problem is F.4.d.
Termination of the Supervisory Relationship:

> Supervisors or supervisees have the right to terminate the super-
> visory relationship with adequate notice. Reasons for withdrawal
> are provided to the other party. When cultural, clinical, or profes-
> sional issues are crucial to the viability of the supervisory relation-
> ships, both parties make efforts to resolve these differences. When

termination is warranted, supervisors make appropriate referrals to possible alternative supervisors.

The above situation illustrates the confounding problems that evolve from a poor supervisor/supervisee match. The supervisee had some specific expectations for her supervision but contracted for services knowing this supervisor did not meet them. When they ran into problems, the supervisor seemed oblivious to the supervisee's frustration but neither did she voice her concerns. Instead the supervisor presumed all was well and the supervisee decided to end the relationship. This too was handled indirectly, with the supervisor thinking it was a gender issue when it appears to have been a professional courtesy and theoretical orientation issue. While the supervisee was within her rights to terminate the supervision, this was not done after a genuine attempt to discuss and resolve the differences. The supervisor was not given any feedback or offered an opportunity to change his behavior and he could not give the supervisee an appropriate referral to another supervisor. It would have been better for the supervisee to address the supervisor's tardiness and her dissatisfaction with his theoretical orientation. The termination may still have occurred but both would have been informed and involved in the process.

You Can't Change What You're Not Aware Of

A newly graduated master's degree therapist took a job with an area agency. The therapist arrived with strong recommendations from his graduate program and even stronger recommendations from his internship supervisor. He was given an adequate orientation to his new job and was informed about the performance evaluation process. As the weeks turned into months, the therapist thought he was doing well. Yes, he had made a few mistakes but these were caught and corrected. Overall, he had the impression all was going well. Then near the end of his sixth month review he was unexpectedly fired. The reasons given were well beyond the mistakes that were previously brought to his attention. They included concern about his attitude, clinical judgment, and ethical decision making. He was shocked and hurt. He had met frequently with his clinical supervisor but none of these issues were ever brought up. He felt betrayed and angry.

Discussion Questions #10:

1. Is it realistic to expect a new professional to make some mistakes?

_____

_____

_____

_____

2. Should a counselor be informed of all their shortcomings?

_____

_____

_____

_____

3. Is it the supervisor's responsibility to outline corrective action?

_____

_____

_____

_____

4. Is it legal for an employer to terminate an employee without disclosure of cause?

_____

_____

_____

_____

5. Is it ethical for a supervisor to dismiss a counselor without feedback or without referral for reparative measures?

_____

_____

_____

_____

The ACA (2014) guideline that relates to this problem is F.5.a. Evaluation and F.5.b. Limitations:

> Supervisors document and provide supervisees with ongoing performance appraisal and evaluation feedback and schedule periodic formal evaluative sessions throughout the supervisory relationship. Through ongoing evaluation and appraisal, supervisors are aware of the limitations of supervisees that might impede performance. Supervisors assist supervisees in securing remedial assistance when needed. They recommend dismissal from training programs, applied counseling settings, or state or voluntary professional credentialing processes when those supervisees are unable to provide competent professional services.

New professionals are likely to make mistakes. This is generally an opportunity for feedback, education, and further training rather than judgment, punishment, or dismissal. Having said this, all supervisors must oversee and guard the competence of their supervisee's performance. Clients' welfare and institutional liability is at stake. Adequate oversight is best accomplished through a program of frequent review, evaluation, feedback, and documentation. Should remedial work be required, a supervisor is responsible for offering referrals for such assistance. In the above situation, the supervisee was not fully informed of the problems with his performance and was not offered an opportunity to remedy those problems. Should his problems have significantly impaired his therapeutic effectiveness, it may have become necessary for him to be temporarily relieved of his clinical duties. If the incompetence is so severe or if after remediation impairment still persists, it is the supervisor's responsibility to see to it that the supervisee is dismissed from his position. These are often very difficult decisions and may require consultation with another supervisor and proper documentation of the rationale for the disciplinary action. In addition, it is important that the supervisee be apprised of their options to address and/or appeal any such decision. Supervision is the primary mechanism by which we insure clients receive competent therapeutic services. It is also the frontline mechanism whereby clinicians receive the feedback and assistance they need to continue to provide quality service.

From the research by Worthen and Lambert (2007), important contributions may be applied to supervision and training. By providing standardized performance and progress feedback in supervision, counselors in training receive objective and subjective feedback about their skills and treatment. Providing feedback from the client's perspective offers an additional dimension to the feedback. As the authors eloquently stated, "It is the combination of clinical wisdom informed by standardized sources of information that may ultimately contribute to improved outcomes and give us a powerful new focus in supervision" (p. 52).

Counselor Heal Thyself

A graduate professor in a master's degree counseling program supervises several students. She also offers supervision services to community mental health professionals. Sometimes in the course of supervision she becomes aware of supervisee's unresolved personal matters that seem to be negatively affecting their clinical work with clients. When this happens with a student she helps them understand the problem and refers them for personal counseling. She does not want a dual teaching and professional therapy relationship with a student. When this occurs with a community mental health professional, however, she offers the supervisee the opportunity in supervision to work on their personal issues. She feels since they already have good rapport and have an established financial arrangement, it isn't much of a stretch to provide both personal counseling and supervision. In addition, her supervision clients seem to appreciate the convenience of doing both under one roof. All seemed to work well until one case presented a dilemma that neither the supervisee nor supervisor saw coming.

A non-student supervisee was working with an older couple and having some difficulty helping them disengage from constant verbal conflict. He tried many different approaches, several suggested by his supervisor but none was effective. The couple was drifting closer and closer to divorce. The supervisee was very upset by his inability to help this couple. The supervisor recognized this and explored with the counselor why he was so reluctant to accept that perhaps this couple did not want to improve their relationship. During the exploration, the supervisee disclosed he too was struggling with his marriage. His wife wanted out while he wanted to work on it. The supervisor suggested that this might be the reason it is so difficult for him to accept his clients may choose to divorce. As they spoke, the supervisee broke into tears and asked his supervisor if she could provide counseling for his wife and him.

The supervisor agreed. The supervisee and his wife went as a couple for several sessions. Little progress was made. The supervisee's wife still wanted out and the supervisee didn't want to accept it. As his supervisor tried to help him come to accept his marriage was ending, the supervisee became very angry and blamed his supervisor for not trying hard enough. The supervisor apologized for being unable to help his supervisee save his marriage but this didn't stop the supervisee from losing trust and respect in his supervisor. Their supervision was never the same.

Discussion Questions #11:

1. Is it reasonable to have one policy about providing counseling to student supervisees and another for private pay supervisees?

_____

_____

_____

_____

2. Did the supervisee really need counseling?

_____

_____

_____

_____

3. Are rapport and convenience the only factors to consider in agreeing to counsel a supervisee?

_____

_____

_____

_____

4. How could this supervisor and supervisee salvage their supervision relationship?

_____

_____

_____

_____

5. Why should this supervisor never have agreed to counsel her supervisee?

_____

_____

_____

_____

The ACA (2014) ethical guideline that addresses this issue is F.5.c. Counseling for Supervisees:

> If supervisees request counseling, counseling supervisors provide them with acceptable referrals. Counselors do not provide counseling services to supervisees. Supervisors address interpersonal competencies in terms of the impact of these issues on clients, the supervisory relationship, and professional functioning.

The above situation appears to be advantageous for the supervisee until the counseling fails and the dual role of supervisor and counselor undermine the trust and respect of the supervisory relationship. The supervisor would have been best advised to avoid counseling not only student supervisees but also private pay supervisees. Although it is possible that greed was the supervisor's underlying motive, it is more likely that she was blinded by her well-meaning intention to help the supervisee with his case and his marriage. Sadly, the supervisee lost much more than he likely anticipated. He lost his marriage, therapist, and supervisory relationship. This is an unfortunate example of the serious problem with dual relationships.

Somewhat overshadowed in the above discussion is the issue of the supervisee's need for therapy. It is clear from his struggle with his divorcing clients that this supervisee's difficulty in his own marriage was negatively affecting his therapeutic effectiveness. A referral for counseling does appear warranted. The problem however is: will counseling help him quickly enough to benefit his work with his clients or, given his impairment, is this supervisee better advised to refer these clients to another therapist? This is both a difficult and awkward situation to handle, but one an effective supervisor can readily help resolve. This counselor needs to manage his personal issues in such a manner that they do not cause harm to his clients. Should he refuse to get counseling, an ethical problem does exist. Although not an issue in the above problem, should this supervisee remain impaired, the supervisor is obliged to not endorse him for certification, licensure, employment, or, in the case of a student, completion of an academic training program. This is one of the hardest boundaries to set with a supervisee, be they a student or fellow colleague, but one that is absolutely necessary in order to assure competent professional performance and safeguard client welfare.

Ramos-Sanchez and colleagues (2002) believe in the importance of graduate counseling students seeking out individual therapy. The authors list three areas that may improve through therapy: expand personal awareness, foster personal and professional development, and enhance the supervisory relationship. Haynes et al. (2003) also believe it is appropriate to encourage supervisees to seek counseling. Perhaps if therapy is supported on both ends of the continuum from schooling to supervision, newly trained professionals will emerge healthier, more confident and competent.

The Adventures of an Apprehensive Digital Immigrant

An older adult student, who has decided to change careers in midlife, has enrolled in an online counseling program. While he has general familiarity with computer technology and social media, he is apprehensive about how to successfully navigate all the technological demands of the program, especially those requiring real-time, online interaction with his clinical supervisor. Living in a rural area, he has little access to local technical help and his internet service frequently goes down. In addition, he has concerns about how he will juggle his personal access to the family computer with three teenagers and a wife, who use the computer for school work, gaming, and social media.

Over the next few months, he has learned how to engage the online coursework and has become proficient at email communication with his classmates and teachers. Now he is beginning his clinical work, seeing clients and reviewing cases with his clinical supervisor. It is still a struggle finding time on the family computer, especially in the evenings when everyone is home and wanting to get online. It is important to note that since the kids were young, he and his wife set up the computer in the family room so they could keep a close eye on their computer use. This has worked out very well, but trying to do real-time, online, clinical supervision in the family room with family members popping in and out has become near impossible. Even when the family commotion has settled down and good interaction with his supervisor is possible, the internet sometimes goes down and interrupts the supervision session. Of further concern is his occasional discomfort in talking about client and supervision issues with his family walking in and out of the room. Thus far, he just keeps an eye open for stray family members and pauses his discussion with his supervisor until they are out of ear-shot. As a relative newcomer to computer technology he also struggles with what to him feels like a more impersonal means of communication. He has never met his supervisor in person but has tried to learn more about her by checking out her social media page. His heart seems to be in the right place and his intentions seem good. Still he feels unsettled and apprehensive about his online experience.

Discussion Questions #12:

1. What level of comfort and experience with computer technology is necessary to successfully engage online supervision?

_____

_____

_____

_____

2. What is the supervisor's responsibility in assuring that a prospective online supervisee has the necessary hardware/software capacity, support, and emotional constitution for online supervision?

_____

_____

_____

_____

3. What are the essential home and/or work environmental factors necessary to ensure privacy and confidentiality of clinical supervision?

_____

_____

_____

_____

4. How important are the relational aspects of clinical supervision and how can these be best facilitated online?

_____

_____

_____

_____

Marc Prensky (2001) first coined the terms digital immigrant and digital native to differentiate the relative discomfort and lack of experience earlier generations, which have not grown up with computer technology, may have with its use in education, work, or leisure activities. With the continued dramatic shift from a manufacturing to a service economy, older generations that seek re-education may find themselves inherently unfamiliar and uncomfortable with the myriad of applications of computer technology and social media. While younger students and professionals may readily accept and thrive in the digital world, older students and professionals may struggle.

The ACA (2014) ethical guidelines state, under Section F Supervision, Training and Teaching:

Counselor supervisors, trainers, and educators aspire to foster meaningful and respectful professional relationships and to maintain appropriate boundaries with supervisees and students in both face-to-face and electronic formats.

Further in Section H Distance Counseling, Technology and Social Media it states:

Counselors understand that the profession of counseling may no longer be limited to in-person, face-to-face interactions. Counselors actively attempt to understand the evolving nature of the profession with regard to distance counseling (and supervision), technology, and social media and how such resources may be used to better serve their clients (and supervisees).

Therefore, when supervisees present with differing levels of comfort and/or experience with online or digital technology, it becomes necessary for the supervisor to acknowledge these needs, explore, through the supervisor responsibility of F.4.a. Informed Consent for Supervision, the potential benefits and limitations of online supervision, and provide mechanisms of technical or personal support for the supervisee. Of further note is research that has compared supervisees' perceptions of effective supervision between fully synchronous cyber-supervision (online) and traditional methods (face to face). In this work, Bender and Dykeman (2016) found no differences in the effectiveness of supervision between the two modalities in a sample of master's level counseling student supervisees. This suggests that the apprehension of the digital immigrant, as it relates to clinical supervision, may be unfounded.

In another study on the effective use of technology in the clinical supervision of health professionals, Martin, Kumar, and Lizarondo (2017) found ten evidence-informed guidelines for supervisors. These further described the supervisory responsibility and included: (1) Set clear expectations and goals; (2) Use a variety of online modalities; (3) Embed supervision into a sound framework of educational principles such as connecting casework to theory, technique, and therapeutic relationship; (4) Focus on the quality of the supervisory relationship; (5) Formulate a plan to manage any technical problems; (6) Pay attention to communication (use of silence, minimize distractions, etiquette, turn-taking, clarity, paraphrasing, and questioning); (7) Rethink notions of continuity and problems of proximity with increased availability; (8) Protect online security, safety, and confidentiality; and (10) Regularly review the online arrangement.

While clinical supervisors and counselor education programs can do much to facilitate a seamless use of digital technology and structure the online supervision session, they cannot as readily control the home or work environment in which the supervisee is accessing the technology. In a study of ethics, relationships, and pragmatics in the use of e-technologies in counseling supervision, three themes emerged (Flanagan, Cottrell, Graham, Marsden, Roberts, & Young, 2017). These included: (1) Secure a sound supervisory relationship by having at least one face-to-face session before beginning online supervision; (2) Be prepared to manage any technological interruptions (processing speed issues, break in connections, software problems, poor image or sound quality problems); and (3) Guard the confidentiality, privacy, and safety of the digital supervisor and supervisee environment. Many ethical issues apply to these concerns.

The ACA (2014) ethical code H.2 Informed Consent and Security for Distance Counseling, Technology and Social Media, spells out under H.2.a. Informed Consent and Disclosure that several issues, such as risks and benefits of technology use, possibility of technology failure, alternate methods of service delivery, handling of emergency problems, and time zone differences, should be discussed upfront. It further explains, under H.2.b. Confidentiality Maintained by the Counselor, H.2.c. Acknowledgment of Limitations, and H.2.d. Security, that while confidentiality should be maintained there may be real limits to maintaining the confidentiality of electronic records and transmissions as these may relate to colleagues, supervisors, information technologists, employees, and other potentially unauthorized access. While encryption may help safeguard access to digital information, the use of firewalls, passwords, and automatic deletion periods that destroy data after a given period may further manage unauthorized access to confidential information. Also note that other forms of electronic or digital information must also be protected including: telephone and conference calls, social media notifications, audio and video communication, and information backed up on data storage devices.

These technical mechanisms of course do not eliminate the possibility of human factors impacting confidentiality, privacy, and safety. In the above case, the supervisee is using the family computer in the family room with other family members within ear-shot. Of course the supervisee should be advised to relocate the computer from the family room to a more private setting, or better yet, purchase a separate, dedicated computer for their confidential and private educational and supervisory use.

Finally, to help create a more personal relationship with his supervisor, the supervisee attempted to interact with the supervisor on social media. The ACA code H.6. Social Media, states in H.6.a. Virtual Professional Presence, that counselors (supervisors) should maintain a separate professional and personal web page, in H.6.b. Social Media as Part of Informed Consent, should inform their clients (supervisees) of the boundaries in the use of social media, and in H.6.c. Client Virtual Presence, respect the privacy of clients' (supervisees') presence on social media. Although the supervisee's efforts to reach out to the supervisor appear to have been intended to improve their interpersonal relationship, this may have been better addressed during a supervision session. Doing so could have allowed the supervisor an opportunity to address the issue directly and remind the supervisee of the limits of their professional boundaries as it relates to social media.

Digital and online technology provide distinct advantages for the effective provision of distance clinical supervision. Harnessing those advantages for both the digital immigrant and digital native can assist both in receiving a meaningful supervision experience. For more information on the use of technology to enhance clinical supervision, please refer to the comprehensive resource, *Using Technology to Enhance Clinical Supervision*, edited by Rousmaniere and Renfro-Michel (2016).

How Should You Respond to an Ethical Complaint?

It is important to first understand that the primary purpose of a credentialing or licensing review board is consumer protection, and this carries with it obvious legal, professional, and ethical implications. Credentialing boards such as the Center for Credentialing and Education (2019), National Board of Certified Counselors (2019), and state licensing review boards enforce a set of standards that have been either set forth by a professional organization or put into law by a state legislature. The board's charge is the oversight of the competent provision of professional services. To accomplish this, they typically review the credentials of all applicants, often require testing of basic professional and practice knowledge, and review and act on any complaints brought forth against any of their certified or licensed providers. While most professionals understand and accept the value of credential review and testing, the prospect of facing a complaint raises much anxiety.

Complaints can be presented to a review board from many sources including employers, supervisors, colleagues, and clients. Most ethical guidelines outline a procedure for initial resolution of a complaint through direct discussion with the offending party. In this way misunderstanding, feedback, and corrective action can be immediately taken. However when the offending behavior is more egregious, the initial attempt at resolution is met with a defensive response, and the inappropriate behavior persists, then a complaint is very likely to be filed with a credentialing or licensing review board. The board's responsibility is to then investigate the complaint, determine whether it warrants corrective or disciplinary action, decide what action should be taken, and follow up on compliance with its requirements.

Most complaints brought to a review board are resolved through remediation, requiring additional training or specialized supervision. Other complaints are met with some form of censure, ranging from placement on probation, to temporary or permanent loss of a license or certification. This is the source of most practitioners' fear. Will I be reprimanded? Will I be censured? Will I lose my certification or license? Will I be unable to practice my profession? It is no doubt embarrassing and humiliating to be the focus of a complaint but it is unwise to become defensive and assume the worst.

We are all human beings and as such are capable of making mistakes. Being informed and conscientious about the ethical guidelines of practice and participating in ongoing supervision can go a long way in limiting the potential for complaints. However, should you still become the focus of a complaint remember the review board is protecting the consumer and guarding the profession. Be honest in the investigation. Accept responsibility for your actions. Be open to the feedback you receive. If you are given remedial requirements to fulfill, accept them as a learning opportunity and a means to improve your skills. If you are censured, deeply reflect upon your actions and either recommit to your profession and do all that is necessary to re-establish your good standing or accept that this profession may not be for you and refocus on a new career. It is never easy to be the focus of a review board complaint, but it can be a critical and beneficial life-changing experience.

Discussion Questions #13:

1. What are your biggest concerns about entering into a personal counseling relationship?

_____

_____

_____

_____

2. What lessons may be learned if a complaint/grievance is filed against you?

_____

_____

_____

_____

Neurocounseling and Its Implications for Ethical Supervision

In this chapter, ethical dilemmas and constructs were presented and discussed. You were challenged to discern the best possible outcomes using ethical guidelines and supervision. It is also essential to better understand where in the brain much ethical behavior may occur. Look at the Head Map of Function (Figure 2.1 in Chapter Two) and locate Fp2 on the right side of the head. This site, plus a few others, are responsible for impulse control, making healthy judgment calls, and even our awareness of many social cues and occurrences. During supervision when a supervisee consults with the supervisor on an area of conflict, ethics, and possible solutions, Fp2 is being activated and strengthened. Remember neurons that fire together, wire together. The more you use ethical decision making, the more you strengthen the prefrontal cortex, especially Fp2.

Summary

The challenges of counseling supervision can be best met through the guidance offered by a set of detailed ethical principles for professional conduct. The strongest supervisor/supervisee relationships provide a meaningful and respectful partnership that enhances both professional practice and client care. This chapter reviewed the ACA Ethical Principles as they apply to counselor supervision. These emphasized that the professional counselor's primary responsibility remains the welfare of their clients. All clients should be informed about their counselor's status as a supervisee and full disclosure should be made as to how the clients' personal information will be shared in supervision. The principles also stated counseling supervisors should be specially trained and supervised to assure the quality and effectiveness of their supervision. Conflict of roles and dual relationships should be limited and if possible avoided because they have the very real potential of undermining one another. This however does not mean that supervisors cannot participate in potentially beneficial relationships with supervisees, such as weddings, funerals, professional meetings, or training seminars.

This chapter also stressed that supervisees should be fully informed of the standards of success, evaluation procedures, job orientation, and any appeal processes that may be in place to challenge an unfair supervisory action. The ACA ethics further recognized that sometimes supervisor/supervisee relationships must be terminated but this should be done after attempts to resolve conflicts have failed and both parties have understood and agreed to this remedy. Perhaps most difficult, supervisors should be honest and accurate in their evaluation of supervisee limitations even if this means the supervisee may not pass their class, fulfill workplace requirements, or qualify for certification and/or licensure. In the case of an impaired supervisee, the supervisee should be referred for remediation (counseling) and not treated by the supervisor, as this will constitute a dual relationship and present a conflict of interest for the supervisor. This chapter outlined the purpose of certification and licensure review boards and the important charge they have to protect the consumer and guard the profession. Although difficult to face a complaint and the possibility of remediation or censure, it is the professional counselor's responsibility to provide competent service and do all they can to bring unethical behavior problems into appropriate ethical compliance. Finally, integration of neurocounseling into ethics and supervision illustrates how and where ethical decisions are often made in the brain. The Fp2 brain site is one area and function helping us to make ethical decisions.

References

American Counseling Association (ACA) (2014). ACA code of ethics and standards of practice. Alexandria, VA: Author.

American Mental Health Counselors Association (AMHCA) (2015). Code of ethics of the American Mental Health Counselors Association. Alexandria, VA: Author.

American Psychological Association (APA) (2017). APA code of ethics and conduct. Washington, DC: Author.

Association for Counselor Education and Supervision (2005). ACES code of ethics for counseling supervision. Alexandria, VA: Author.

Baird, B.N. (2002). *The internship, practicum, and field placement handbook: A guide for the helping professional* (3rd ed.). Upper Saddle River, NJ: Prentice Hall.

Bender, S. & Dykeman, C. (2016). Supervisees' perceptions of effective supervision: A comparison of fully synchronous cybersupervision to traditional methods. *Journal of Technology in Human Services*, 34(4). https://doi.org/10.1080/15228835.2016.1250026

Center for Credentialing and Education (CCE) (2019). Greensboro, NC: Author.

Cobia, D.C. & Boes, S.R. (2000). Professional disclosure statements and formal plans for supervision: Two strategies for minimizing the risk of ethical conflicts in post-master's supervision. *Journal of Counseling and Development*, 78(3), 293–296.

Corey, G., Corey, M.S., & Callanan, P. (2003). *Issues and ethics in the helping professions* (6th ed.). Pacific Grove, CA: Brooks/Cole.

Flanagan, P., Cottrell, C., Graham, H., Marsden, V., Roberts, L., & Young, J. (2017). Ethics, relationships and pragmatics in the use of e-technologies in counselling supervision. *New Zealand Journal of Counselling*, 37(1), 24–43.

Garb, H.N. (2005). Clinical judgment and decision making. *Annual Review of Clinical Psychology*, 55, 310–323.

Hannan, C., Lambert, M.J., Harmon, C., Nielsen, S.L., Smart, D.W., & Shimokawa, K. (2005). A lab test and algorithms for identifying clients at risk for treatment failure. *Journal of Clinical Psychology/In session*, 61, 1–9.

Haynes, R., Corey, G., & Moulton, P. (2003). *Clinical supervision in the helping professions: A practical guide*. Pacific Grove, CA: Brooks/Cole.

Kaplan, D. (2003). Excellence in ethics. *Counseling Today*, 45(10), 5.

Kwan, K.K. (2001). Models of racial and ethnic identity development: Delineation of practical implications. *Journal of Mental Health Counseling*, 23, 269–277.

Martin, P., Kumar, S., & Lizarondo, L. (2017). Effective use of technology in clinical supervision. *Internet Intervention*, 8, 35–39. https://doi.org/10.1016/j.invent.2017.03.001.

National Association of Social Workers (NASW) (2017). Code of ethics. Washington, DC: NASW Press.

National Board of Certified Counselors (2019). Alexandria, VA.

Polanski, P. (2000). Training supervisors at the master's level: Developmental considerations. *ACES Spectrum Newsletter*, 61(2), 3–5.

Prensky, M. (2001). Digital natives, digital immigrants. *On the Horizon*, 9(5), 1–6. doi.10.1108/10748120110424816.

Ramos-Sanchez, L., Esnil, G., Goodwin, A., Riggs, S., Touster, L.O., Wright, L.K., et al. (2002). Negative supervisory events: Effects on supervision satisfaction and supervisory alliance. *Professional Psychology, Research and Practice*, 33(2), 197–202.

Rousmaniere, T. & Renfro-Michel, E. (2016). *Using Technology to Enhance Clinical Supervision*. Alexandria, VA: American Counseling Association.

Russell-Chapin, L.A., Sherman, N., & Ivey, A.E. (2016). *Your supervised practicum and internship: Field resources for turning theory into practice* (2nd ed.). New York, NY: Routledge.

Russell-Chapin, L.A. & Ivey, A.E. (2004). *Your supervised practicum and internship: Field resources for turning theory into practice*. Pacific Grove: CA, Brooks/Cole.

Sue, D.W., Arredondo, P., & McDavis, R.J. (1992). Multicultural competencies/standards: A call to the profession. *Journal of Counseling and Development*, 70, 477–486.

Sumerel, M.B. & Borders, L.D. (1996). Addressing personal issues in supervision: Impact on counselors' experience level on various aspects of the supervisory relationship. *Counselor Education and Supervision*, 35(4), 268–286.

Williamson, J.N. & Williamson, D. (2018). Beginning with the end in mind: Precommitment considerations for the supervisory relationship. *Counseling Today*, American Counseling Association, July, 12–14.

Worthen, V.E. & Lambert, J. (2007). Outcome oriented supervision: Advantages of adding systematic client tracking to supportive consultations. *Counselling and Psychotherapy Research*, 7(1), 48–53.

APPENDIX 3.A WEB ADDRESSES FOR PROFESSIONAL ORGANIZATIONS AND CODES OF ETHICS

American Association of Christian Counselors: Code of Ethics
www.aacc.net/

American Association of Marriage and Family Therapy: Code of Ethics
https://www.aamft.org/

American Association of Pastoral Counselors: Code of Ethics
https://www.acpe.edu/ACPE/Psychotherapy/Psychotherapy.aspx

American Counseling Association: Code of Ethics and Standards of Practice:
www.counseling.org/resources/codeofethics

American Group Psychotherapy Association: Guidelines for Ethics
www.groupsinc.org/group/ethicalguide.html

American Medical Association: Principles of Ethics
www.ama-assn.org

American Psychoanalytic Association: Principles and Standards of Ethics for Psychoanalysts
http://www.apsa.org/

American Psychological Association: Ethical Principles and Code of Conduct
www.apa.org/ethics/code.html

American School Counseling Association: Principles for Professional Ethics
www.schoolcounselor.org

Australian Psychological Society: Code of Ethics
www.psychsociety.com.au/about/finalcode.pdf

British Association for Counselling: Code of Ethics and Practice for Counsellors
https://www.bacp.co.uk/

Canadian Counselling Association: Codes of Ethics
https://www.cpca-rpc.ca/code-of-ethics~.aspx

Canadian Psychological Association
www.cpa.ca

Commission on Rehabilitation Counselor Certification: Code of Professional Ethics
https://www.crccertification.com/

National Association of Alcoholism and Drug Abuse Counselors: Ethical Standards
http://naadac.org/ethics

National Organization for Human Service Education: Ethical Standards
https://www.nationalhumanservices.org/ethical-standards-for-hs-professionals

National Association of Social Workers: Code of Ethics
www.socialworkers.org/pubs/code/default

National Board for Certified Counselors: Code of Ethics
www.nbcc.org/ethics

New Zealand Association of Counsellors Inc.: Code of Ethics
http://www.nzac.org.nz/code_of_ethics.cfm

4
DEVELOPMENTAL SUPERVISION MODELS

Overview

Before beginning the chapters on different types of supervision models, this chapter will offer a common-factor approach to supervision, identifying common elements throughout all supervision models. Then the chapter will provide an overview of developmental models of supervision. Developmental supervision models tend to be flexible based upon the supervisee's needs and outcomes. The basic tenets and stages will be discussed emphasizing supervisee levels of functioning and supervisor's possible interventions and responses. Follow along using the transcription guide in this chapter, as you watch the video demonstration using a development supervision model. Reflection questions are at the end of the chapter to allow the reader integration of the concepts. A section on neurocounseling and its implications to supervision will discuss the importance of a therapeutic and supervisory relationship to the social brain and the polyvagal theory.

Goals

- Understand the benefits of a common-factor approach to supervision.
- Define the needs of each supervisee in differing developmental stages.

- Understand the appropriate supervisory response and behaviors of each stage.
- Identify when developmental models might be selected for supervision.
- Integrate the social brain, physiology, and emotional safety to the supervision process.

Common Factors Approach to Supervision

Morgan and Sprenkle (2007) took on the enormous task of looking at the majority of supervision models, theories, and skills in order to identify a common set of supervision practices. From their literature review general supervision constructs were recognized.

- Supervision involves a relationship between a supervisor with greater experience in counseling and a supervisee with lesser experience.
- Supervision involves a structured relationship between the supervisor and supervisee with the goal of helping the supervisee to gain the attitude, skills, and knowledge to become an effective helping professional.
- Common supervision domains are relevant: development of clinical skills, theories and client dynamics, professional and ethical behaviors, personal growth of the supervisee, autonomy and confidence levels, and monitoring and evaluation of the supervisee.

The literature review produced a first list of 238 supervisor behaviors, so after no new activities or domains appeared, the authors developed a three-dimensional approach to supervision using three continua and four supervisor roles. This conceptual model may assist all supervisors in combining common practices with preferred, specific models.

The first continuum focuses on the supervisory emphasis from clinical issues and competency such as clinical skills and theories on one end to professional competency on the other end, such as personal growth, ethics, and professionalism.

The second continuum emphasizes the various levels of specificity of a supervisor from idiosyncratic/particular on the left end of the continuum to nomothetic/general on the right end. It is the supervisor's responsibility to focus on one or both of the supervisee's individual needs and the profession's needs.

The third and final continuum concerns the supervisory relationship. This continuum is related more on how supervisors do their jobs rather than what they do. This relationship continuum can be collaborative on the right end to directive on the left end.

The authors summarize their common-factor supervision approach by describing that the content of supervision, the actions of supervisors and what they do, can be illustrated by the first two continua: emphasis and specificity. The final continuum/dimension focuses on the nature of the supervisory relationship. Within these dimensions four supervisory roles can be seen: coach, teacher, administrator, and mentor (see Figure 4.1).

Morgan and Sprenkle (2007) state,

We are not, therefore, suggesting that supervisors drop their models and merely employ the common factors. Rather, the field is

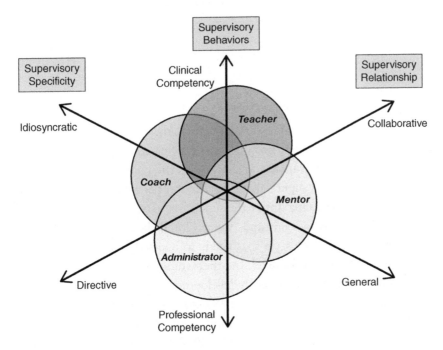

Figure 4.1 Common Factors Approach for Supervision
Source: ©Pearson 2014 as per Bradley & Pearson Partnership

likely to benefit most from a both/and attitude toward specific models and common factors. As has been suggested for clinical common factors, we believe that specific models are the medium through which the common factors work (Sprenkle and Blow, 2004), and which provide the variety and diversity needed to match human complexity. (p. 7)

As the reader continues through the supervision model journey and begins to find the "best fit" for the supervisor and supervisee, remember to use the common factors approach plus differing supervision models. They are interwoven one with the other.

Discussion Question #1:

1. What may be the benefits of using a common factors approach to better understanding the complexity of supervision?

_____

_____

_____

_____

Developmental Models of Supervision

The basic tenets formulating developmental models of supervision are that supervisees continue to grow at individual paces with differing needs and differing styles of learning. If this is true, then one of the major goals during developmental supervision is to discover personal needs and focus on whatever it takes to maximize the supervisee's strengths and minimize liabilities. In a study by Hart and Nance (2003) the authors found there is an optimal supervisor style that needs to be used for each supervisee developmental level and/or need. In other words there is a certain level of directiveness and support for each development level.

Holloway (1995) writes of at least 18 developmental models. Some examples of different developmental models are Ronnestad and Skovholt (2003), Stoltenberg (1981), and Taibbi (1990). According to these models, in order to manage this developmental nature of learning, the manner in which the supervisee and supervisor interact must also change

(Russell-Chapin & Ivey, 2004). As the supervisees mature and grow, their needs and wants from the supervisor will also change. In individual counseling, assessing the developmental level of the client and choosing a corresponding intervention is essential. A similar parallel process occurs within developmental supervision (Russell-Chapin, 2007). Two examples of developmental models will be explored.

Stoltenberg, McNeill, and Delworth's Developmental Supervision Model

Stoltenberg (1981), Stoltenberg and Delworth (1987), and Stoltenberg, McNeill, and Delworth (1998) formulated a Developmental Supervision Model describing distinct levels of supervisees: beginning, intermediate, advanced, and master counselor. During each level or stage, the job of the supervisor would be to structure supervision moving from imitative and demonstrative functions at the beginning level to more competent and self-reliant functions during the advanced levels (Stoltenberg, McNeill, & Delworth, 1998).

McNeill and Stoltenberg (2016) added to the original model by suggesting that clinical supervision is critical to the outcome of therapy. Within the first 15 years of helping professionals' practice, 85–90 percent will become supervisors. It is imperative that supervisory skills are taught in graduate curricula.

Therefore, in this model a strong emphasis is on the supervisee's ability to better understand self and others, and their motivational levels and ability to become autonomous. Each level includes those three processes (awareness, motivation, and autonomy), and within each level are nine growth areas to emphasize. See Table 4.1 to better understand each level.

The nine growth areas are: intervention, skill competence, assessment techniques, interpersonal assessment, client conceptualization, individual differences, theoretical orientation, treatment goals and plans, and professional ethics. In developmental supervision, the job of the supervisor and supervisee will be to help the supervisee discover personal strengths areas for improvement. This strategy can be a lifelong learning pattern, and as a helping professional, it can be responsible for personal growth throughout a helping profession. Table 4.1 lists the behaviors of the supervisee and the supervisor.

Table 4.1 Behaviors of Supervisees and Supervisors

Levels	Behavior of Supervisee	Behavior of Supervisor
Beginning-Level 1	Little experience; dependent on the supervisor	Models needed skills and behaviors; teacher role
Intermediate-Level 2	Less imitative; strives for independence	Provides some structure but encourages exploration
Advanced-Level 3	More insightful and motivated; more autonomous sharing	Listens and offers suggestions when asked
Master Counselor-Level 4	Skilled interpersonally, cognitively, and professionally	Provides collegial and consultative functions

Basic Tenet

Supervisees grow at individual paces with differing needs and styles of learning often with stages of growth that are dependent upon skill level and need of the client.

When to Use

Use this model when assessment of the developmental level of the supervisee is needed.

Supervisor's Emphasis and Goals

- Assess the supervisee's developmental level of functioning from levels 1 through 4
- Understand the supervisee's world, motivational levels, and degree of autonomy
- Identify needed growth areas in each of the four levels using the nine intervention areas listed below.

Supervisee Growth Areas

1. Interventions
2. Skill Competence
3. Assessment Techniques
4. Interpersonal Assessment
5. Client Conceptualization
6. Individual Differences
7. Theoretical Orientation
8. Treatment Goals and Plans
9. Professional Ethics.

Limitations

This model does not go deep enough into specific supervision methods for each supervisee level, and it focuses only on student development as supervisees (Haynes, Corey, & Moulton, 2003). Additionally, in a study of 100 supervisees, Ladany, Marotta, and Muse-Burke (2001) found no differences of supervisees' preferences based on experience levels. The authors write that developmental assumptions may be "based more on clinical lore than on research" (p. 215). Storm, Todd, Sprenkle, and Morgan (2001) found little empirical evidence to support the developmental assumptions.

Discussion Questions #2:

1. How might this developmental model assist you as a supervisee and supervisor?

   _____

   _____

   _____

   _____

2. How will this developmental model assist you as a supervisor?

   _____

   _____

   _____

   _____

3. What are your concerns about this developmental supervision model?

   _____

   _____

   _____

   _____

Hersey, Blanchard, and Johnson's Developmental Supervision Model

In addition to supervisees going through different developmental stages depending on supervisory needs, Loganbill, Hardy, and Delworth (1982) believe it is important to assess that same developmental level knowing it may require a differing type of supervisory response.

Hersey, Blanchard, and Johnson (2000) expanded that concept using developmental or maturity level into four differing styles: structured, encouraging, coaching, and mentoring. Again for each level of developmental maturity, the supervisor will respond accordingly. In the Maturity Stage 1(M1), the supervisee might tell the supervisor that he doesn't know exactly what to do with this client. A M1 supervisory response may be to explain in structured detail what to do. In the M2 stage, the supervisee may tell the supervisor that she is working with a client and has conceptualized the case like this. A M2 supervisory response is, "You have worked hard on this case and thought it out thoroughly; I like how you stated your treatment goals." In the M3 stage, the supervisor is excited to share the details on the case and request additional ideas. A M3 supervisory response may sound like, "Using the intentional skill of self-disclosure seemed to work, but have you thought about how it changed the focus of the session?" In the final stage of M4, the supervisee states confidently to the supervisor how the case is developing. The supervisee has very few questions. A M4 supervisory response is, "It is fun to share cases and hear how others intervene" (Russell-Chapin & Ivey, 2004).

Basic Tenet

Just as clients' developmental level is assessed, so must the supervisee's developmental level be assessed with correlating supervisory responses.

When to Use

Use this model when the supervisee's comments and questions indicate hints of the supervisee's developmental level.

Supervisor's Emphasis and Goals

The supervisor responds to the *differing needs and confidence levels*.

Supervisee Growth Areas

Supervisee's questions and comments will demonstrate growing confidence and corresponding maturity levels.

Limitations

The depth of this supervision model may be limited. Additional models may be needed to cover all the comprehensive supervision needs.

Discussion Question #3:

1. What words and phrases could indicate M1, M2, M3, and M4 developmental levels?

_____

_____

_____

_____

Video Supervisory Question:

Each supervisee in the video demonstration is asked what he/she wants out of the supervision session. The supervision question is the first step in determining which supervision model is needed. The supervision question for this chapter is "When and how do I fit Dad in, so she can be comfortable? How do I get more information for this young woman?"

Developmental Supervision and the Case of Ella

In supervising Ella, Lori listened to her case presentation, the diagnosis, and her supervision question. The selection of Stoltenberg's (1981) and Stoltenberg, McNeill, and Delworth's Developmental Supervision Model (1998) seemed like a wise fit. Lori first assessed Ella's level of functioning from Level 1 through 4. She looked at Ella's awareness of self and others, her motivation toward the developmental process and independent thinking ability. From the supervision question, her ability to articulate the problem and general skills, Ella seemed to be functioning at Level 4. To offer Ella collegial supervision was easy and very interactive. Lori was able to offer Ella possible suggestions, and she was amenable to many of the ideas.

Neurocounseling and Its Implications for Therapeutic Alliance

In this chapter, different types of developmental supervision models were presented with the one developmental supervision model demonstrated through video. These models emphasize the importance of supervisory relationships and rapport building. Understanding our social brain is of utmost importance to supervision and counseling.

The Polyvagal Theory developed by Stephen Porges researches, teaches, and emphasizes the importance of the social brain and emotional safety (2011). All human beings and especially novice counselors and supervisees need to feel safe in the supervisory relationship to engage in constructive feedback and growth.

The vagus nerve is the tenth cranial nerve starting at the base of the medulla oblongata and ending at the abdomen. This longest cranial nerve is responsible for interfacing the brain with other aspects of the body. In this case, the vagus nerve assists with both sensory and motor functions and helps with adaptive abilities to stress in the autonomic nervous system (ANS). You may be familiar with these stages, from the oldest, immobilization or freezing, which relies on the unmyelinated dorsal motor nucleus. The second level in the evolutionary nature is the ubiquitous flight-or-fight reaction using the sympathetic nervous system (SNS).

The third evolutionary level is the social engagement system relying on the myelinated portion of the vagus system. This is essential to supervision as it utilizes voice intonation, facial expression, and all those microcounseling skills for active listening. When a supervisee sees and feels safety, the SNS is deactivated, and the parasympathetic nervous system can take over. This is where self-regulation can begin as well as a healthy supervision process.

Summary

The developmental models have similarities and differences from other models. As the reader continues with each supervision model, look for those concepts that are unique and some that are common. Continue to discover which models seem to best fit the supervisors', supervisees', and clients' needs. You may find that each model has something to offer supervisors and your supervisees. Remember that developmental models allow the supervisor to respond flexibly depending where the supervisee's needs are and offer specific supervisee interventions for each level of functioning.

Chapter Four Final Discussion Questions:

1. Based on Ella's supervision question and her case presentation, why did Lori select the Stoltenberg, McNeill, and Delworth Development

Supervision Model for this supervision session? Go back into the chapter for possible reasons.

_____

_____

_____

_____

2. What are the strengths of this model for a supervisor?

_____

_____

_____

_____

3. What are the strengths of the developmental model as a supervisee?

_____

_____

_____

_____

4. When do you think a developmental supervision model may best serve you?

_____

_____

_____

_____

5. How does better understanding emotional safety and the vagus nerve assist supervisors in developing therapeutic alliance?

_____

_____

_____

_____

References

Hart, G.M. & Nance, D. (2003). Styles of counselor supervision as perceived by supervisors and supervisees. *Counselor Education and Supervision*, 43, 146–158.

Haynes, R., Corey, G., & Moulton, P. (2003). *Clinical supervision in the helping professions: A practical guide*. Pacific Grove, CA: Brooks/Cole.

Hersey, P., Blanchard, K., & Johnson, D. (2000). *Management of organizational behavior: Leading human resources* (8th ed.). Upper Saddle River, NJ: Prentice Hall.

Holloway, E.L. (1995). *Clinical supervision: A systems approach*. Thousand Oaks, CA: Sage.

Ladany, N., Marotta, S., & Muse-Burke, J.L. (2001). Counselor experience related to complexity of case conceptualization and supervision preference. *Counselor Education and Supervision*, 40, 203–219.

Loganbill, C., Hardy, E., & Delworth, U. (1982). Supervision: A conceptual model. *The Counseling Psychologist*, 10, 3–42.

McNeill, B.W. & Stoltenberg, C.D. (2016). *Supervision essentials for the integrative developmental model*. Washington, DC: American Psychological Association.

McNeill, B.W., Stoltenberg, C.D., & Romans, J.S. (1992). The integrated developmental model of supervision: Scale development and validation procedures. *Professional Psychology, Research & Practice*, 23, 504–508.

Morgan, M.M. & Sprenkle, D.H. (2007). Toward a common-factors approach to supervision. *Journal of Marital and Family Therapy*, 33(1), 1–17.

Porges, S. (2011). *The polyvagal theory: Neurological foundations of emotions, attachment, communication & self-regulation*. New York, NY: Norton.

Ronnestad, M.H. & Skovholt, T.M. (2003). The journey of the counselor and therapist: Research findings and perspectives on professional development. *Journal of Career Development*, 30, 5–44.

Russell-Chapin, L.A. (2007). Supervision: An essential for professional counselor development. In J. Gregoire & C.M. Jungers (Eds.), *The counselor's companion: What every beginning counselor needs to know*. Mahwah, NJ: Lawrence Erlbaum.

Russell-Chapin, L.A. & Ivey, A.E. (2004). *Your supervised practicum and internship: Field resources for turning theory into action*. Pacific Grove, CA: Brooks/Cole.

Skovholt, T.M. & Ronnestad, M.H. (1992*). The evolving professional self: Stages and themes in therapists and counselor development*. Chichester, England: Wiley.

Sprenkle, D.H. & Blow, A.J. (2004). Common factors and our sacred models. *Journal of Marital and Family Therapy*, 30, 113–129.

Stoltenberg, C.D. (1981). Approaching supervision from a developmental perspective: The counselor-complexity model. *Journal of Counseling Psychology*, 28, 59–65.

Stoltenberg, C.D., McNeill, B.W., & Delworth, U. (1998). *IDM supervision: An integrated developmental model for supervising counselors and therapists*. San Francisco: Jossey-Bass.

Stoltenberg, C.D. & Delworth, U. (1987). *Supervising counselors and therapists*. San Francisco: Jossey-Bass.

Storm, C.L., Todd, T.C., Sprenkle, D.H., & Morgan, M.M. (2001). Gaps between MFT supervision assumptions and common practice: Suggest best practices. *Journal of Marital and Family Therapy*, 27, 227–239.

Taibbi, R. (1990). Integrated family therapy: A model for supervision. *Families in Society*, 71, 542–549.

5
THEORETICAL-SPECIFIC
SUPERVISION MODELS

Overview

This chapter focuses on the advantages and disadvantages of using theoretical-specific supervision models. The supervisor needs to be familiar with the chosen counseling theory in order to assist the supervisee in expanding technical skills. Five different psychotherapy-based supervision models will be illustrated. Again use the transcription in this chapter as you watch the video demonstration emphasizing a Psychodynamic Supervision Model. Refer to the reflection questions for integration of the neurocounseling concept of homeostatic plasticity and theoretical-specific supervision models.

Goals

- Familiarize supervisors and supervisees with the strengths and liabilities of theoretical-specific supervision models.
- Assist supervisees with possible personal concerns that may interfere with the counseling and supervision process using discipline specific constructs.

Theoretical-specific Supervision

Theoretical-specific or psychotherapy-based supervision uses the tenets, constructs, and theories developed for counseling and change to assist the supervisors with supervision. Therefore, there may be as many theoretical-specific supervision models as there are counseling theories.

Helping professionals who adhere to a specific school of thought and therapy (cognitive behavioral, psychodynamic, Rogerian, etc.) believe that naturally it may be wise to supervise from that same theoretical orientation. The major advantage to the supervisor and supervisee is that if they share the same theoretical orientation, then it maximizes the modeling that can occur in supervision (Bernard & Goodyear, 1998). The supervisor could demonstrate discipline-specific skills as well as integrate necessary theoretical constructs.

A disadvantage may be that the supervisor is not familiar or comfortable enough to model a needed counseling theory. If not, consultation with an expert is required. Another possible liability may be that one theory is too limiting in focus. In addition, from the earliest period of supervision, competent therapists became the supervisors of new trainees. There was little formal training or coursework for supervisors, so clinicians had to apply their belief systems to supervision (White & Russell, 1995). Also what constitutes change in counseling may not be the same for supervision.

There are too many theoretical-specific supervision models to mention them all. Many of the selected models are classic ones. Some continue to thrive and continue to change with outcome research and the times in which we live. Five theoretical supervision models will be examined for our purposes here.

Discussion Question #1:

When would you want supervision to be conducted using a theoretical-specific supervision model?

_____

_____

_____

_____

Woods and Ellis's Rational Emotive Behavioral Supervision Model

If a supervisor viewed Rational Emotive Behavioral Therapy (REBT) as the favored theoretical orientation, then two main skills would be required during supervision. First the supervisor would need to identify the problem and irrational thinking of both the supervisee and the client. Then the supervisee and supervisor would select ways to dispute and challenge those same irrational thoughts as a method for changing and learning new, productive thoughts and behaviors (Ellis, 1989; Woods & Ellis, 1996). A key objective in cognitive behavioral supervision is teaching cognitive behavioral techniques and correcting misconceptions about cognitive behavioral counseling with clients and supervisees (Liese & Beck, 1997). Behavioral and cognitive behavioral supervisors will emphasize and expect the supervisee to demonstrate more technical mastery than most supervisors (Bernard and Goodyear, 1998).

Dryden (2014) states that cognitive behavior therapy is cited most for its evidenced-based treatment strategies. The author continues to share and expand on the first, second, and third waves of REBT. In this thorough and expansive book, Dryden includes many different types of REBT: Dialectical Behavior Therapy, Compassion Focused Therapy, Mindfulness-Based Cognitive Therapy, and Acceptance and Commitment Therapy to name just a few. For further information on cognitive behavioral supervision, peruse the materials from Dryden (2014), Woods and Ellis (1996), and Liese and Beck (1997).

Basic Tenet

The main premise of REBT Supervision is to help the supervisee challenge and dispute any irrational thoughts that may be interfering in the counseling and supervision process.

When to Use

- REBT Supervision is recommended when there is a need for expansion of knowledge of theory and its techniques.
- Continuity and modeling especially in the area of distorted thinking on the part of the supervisee is required.

Supervisor's Roles and Behaviors

- The supervisor's main role is to provide active and direct supervision in accordance with REBT tenets and interventions.
- The supervisor needs to help the supervisee master REBT skills and theoretical understanding.

Supervisor's Emphasis and Goals

The main goal is on technical mastery but not supervisory relationship.

Limitations

Probably the major limitation of REBT Supervision and all theoretical-specific supervision is the narrow focus. The focus, on one hand, may strengthen theoretical skills, but it may also be so specific that the theory excludes other essential components that may well be beneficial to the client and supervisee (Russell-Chapin, 2007; Holloway, 1995).

Discussion Questions #2:

1. What would be the most difficult aspect for you as a supervisor or supervisee using REBT Supervision?

_____

_____

_____

_____

2. As a supervisor, what strategies could you employ to help supervisees work through irrational thoughts?

_____

_____

_____

_____

Rogerian Person-centered Supervision Model

Using supervision from person-centered theory, the supervisor would ensure that the basic facilitative conditions were in process throughout the supervision session. Emphasis would be on unconditional positive regard, building trust, and creating a genuine environment for the supervisee to express self-doubts and fears about confidence in personal counseling skills (Hackney & Goodyear, 1984; Rogers, 1961). The evaluation aspect of supervision is not a main emphasis in person-centered supervision, and Lambers (2000) states that the only agenda is to be fully present and allow the supervisee to be open to the experience with the client. The supervisee's growth potential and self-actualization are the main focus (Haynes, Corey, & Moulton, 2003). For additional information on person-centered supervision, read Patterson (1997) and Lambers (2000).

Basic Tenet

The main tenet is to provide the necessary facilitative conditions for the supervisee to grow and develop into the counselor he/she may become.

When to Use

Rogerian Supervision is selected when the supervisee needs and wants to better understand the experience of the client.

Supervisor's Roles and Behaviors

- The relationship is essential in Rogerian Supervision.
- Nondirective active listening skills are necessary.
- Providing an atmosphere of unconditional positive regard is a foundational element.
- Evaluation is not a critical factor, only the growth of the supervisee as measured by personal insight.

Supervision Emphasis and Goals

The main goal is the supervisee's growth and the better understanding of the client's perspective.

Supervisee Growth Area

Building personal confidence and self-understanding in the counseling process is the main area of growth.

Limitations

Although creating a supervisory atmosphere of safety and trust is helpful to a supervisee, some supervisees may struggle with this nondirective environment. During the early stages in a counseling career, the skill and confidence level may not be secure enough for self-exploration.

Discussion Questions #3:

1. As a supervisor or supervisee, what frustrations might you incur using Rogerian Supervision?

_____

_____

_____

_____

2. What might the supervisee need to self-actualize?

_____

_____

_____

_____

Bradley and Gould's Psychodynamic Supervision Model

In Psychodynamic Supervision, additional emphasis may be on parallel process (Doehrman, 1976). Parallel process is the dynamic that occurs in the client/therapist relationship that is played out in the supervisee/supervisor relationship. The supervisor may focus on the resistance that the supervisee had during the session and investigate what resistance the supervisee may have toward the supervisor. Bradley and Gould (2001) believe that the main goal is to focus on both the intrapersonal and interpersonal dynamics of the supervisee's relationship with everyone whether that be clients, colleagues, and/or friends and family. The textbook authors find that Psychodynamic Supervision may also assist supervisees to make the unconscious conscious allowing them more freedom of choices in counseling and personal living.

Another psychodynamic theory that may assist a supervisee and supervisor is Object Relationship Theory. Walsh (2009) writes, "Object relationship has two meanings." The first meaning "focuses on the quality of our interpersonal relationships. The second focus is on the internalized attitudes towards self and others" (pp. 62–63). Helping the supervisee realize those internalized attitudes and "the power of the situation in the person" (p. 131) may assist the supervisee in better understanding the dynamics created between the client/counselor and supervisee/supervisor. In Psychodynamic Supervision understanding object relationships is essential, as the major goal is to identify the main roles of relationships in the client's life and the supervisee's life. For more in-depth information on Psychodynamic Supervision read Frawley-O'Dea and Sarnat (2001), Haynes, Corey, and Moulton (2003), and Walsh (2009).

Basic Tenet

The basic tenet in Psychodynamic Supervision is the examination of intrapersonal and interpersonal relationships and the parallel process that plays out during the client/counselor interaction and the supervisee/supervisor experience.

When to Use

Psychodynamic Supervision may be selected when the supervisee seems to be "stuck" in the counseling process and showing signs of attraction or dislike for a particular client.

Supervisor's Roles and Behaviors

The supervisor may work on the main constructs of psychodynamic theory such as resistance, transference, and countertransference displayed throughout the counseling and supervision sessions.

Supervision Emphasis and Goals

- The supervisor's main goal is to focus on the supervisee's interpersonal and intrapersonal conflicts in counseling and the supervision process.
- Struggles and patterns with clients, colleagues, supervisors, and family may be explored.

Supervisee Growth Areas

- A primary growth area is the intrapersonal growth of the supervisee.
- Examining possible unconscious motivations underlying counseling choices allows the supervisee more freedom of choice in later counseling and supervision sessions.

Limitations

If Psychodynamic Supervision is the only supervision of choice, it may be possible that the supervisee may grow intrapersonally but not technically.

Discussion Questions #4:

1. How might your own family of origin issues hinder working with the client, supervisee, or supervisor?

_____

_____

_____

_____

2. What kinds of transference and countertransference concerns may inhibit your supervisory process?

_____

_____

_____

_____

Pistole and Fitch's Attachment Theory Supervision Model

Attachment theory in supervision can be especially helpful when the focus is on the supervisory working alliance (Pistole & Fitch, 2008). In Bowlby's (1988) attachment theory the author provides a clear understanding of relational bonding, motivation, affect management, and actions that are pertinent to the supervisor/supervisee relationship. Ladany, Friedlander, and Nelson (2005) identify two essential components in the supervisor/supervisee relationship: the quality of the emotional bond and the supervisor's astuteness to the supervisee's needs (Pistole & Fitch, 2008). It is the supervisor's responsibility to be aware and sensitive to the supervisee's "vulnerability and need for support and reassurance" (Ladany et al., 2005, p. 13). A useful attachment supervision intervention is that of supervisee critical incident. Discussing personal experiences such as deaths, divorce, etc. can activate the attachment system and assist in creating a healthier working alliance. If additional information on attachment theory is warranted, review the works of Mikulincer and Shaver (2007).

Basic Tenet

The main tenet in the Attachment Supervision Model is to focus on the importance of the therapeutic and supervisory working alliances.

When to Use

Attachment Supervision Model is used when the supervisee may be struggling with issues of bonding and motivation.

Supervisor's Roles and Behaviors

The supervisor has an active role in providing interventions that assist the supervisee in discovering awareness into the supervisory process.

Supervision Emphasis and Goals

The main goal is for the supervisor to reassure and encourage the supervisee when counseling and supervision become stressful and awkward.

Supervisee Growth Areas

The supervisee will gain insight and safety throughout the supervision process. This will allow the supervisee to better understand personal attachment patterns that may cloud counseling and supervision outcomes.

Limitations

The focus may be too specific to allow for counseling growth in all areas of counseling and supervision.

Discussion Questions #5:

1. Who in your life has provided the most support for you? How does that impact you? As a supervisor? A supervisee?

_____

_____

_____

_____

2. From your history, to whom have you attached and who has abandoned and neglected you? How does that impact your working alliances with others?

_____

_____

_____

_____

3. What is the pivotal or critical incident in your life that has influenced how you look at relationships in general?

_____

_____

_____

_____

Prouty's Feminist Theory Supervision Model

Feminist Theory of Supervision offers an added depth to supervision and its relationships by emphasizing collaborative and equal partnerships between the supervisor and the supervisee (Prouty, 2001; Morgan & Sprenkle, 2007). The supervisory process and expectations are clearly defined which increases the odds for supervisee participation (Corey, 2001). Haynes, Corey, and Moulton (2003, p. 122) state,

> Although the supervisory relationship cannot be entirely equal, the supervisor shares power in the relationship by creating a collaborative partnership with supervisees. For example, instead of the supervisor providing specific direction to the supervisee, the supervisor can help the supervisee think about his or her clients in new ways, formulate interpretations and devise interventions.

In Prouty's (2001) research five feminist concerns were acknowledged as central features in supervision: gender issues, power inequalities, the role of affect, diversity concerns, and socialization skills. For additional readings on Feminist-based Supervision, see Prouty, Thomas, Johnson, and Long (2001) and Carta-Falsa and Anderson (2001).

Basic Tenet

The main tenet involved in Feminist Supervision is to work together as a supervisory team to collaborate on important supervisory issues.

When to Use

Feminist Supervision is utilized when diversity understanding and power inequities need to be addressed.

Supervisor's Roles and Behaviors

The supervisor's roles are that of equal partner in the supervisory process.

Supervisor's Emphasis and Goals

The main goal is to eliminate the power differential between the supervisee and the supervisor. This equity allows for less insecurity on the supervisee's part and additional opportunities for independence and safety.

Limitations

The Feminist Supervision Model adds an essential layer to supervision by focusing on power, oppression, and diversity concerns. However, all aspects of counseling competency need to be addressed to ensure supervision efficacy.

Discussion Questions #6:

1. How may your beliefs about gender roles influence the way you interact in supervision?

2. What would it look like during a supervision session, if there were power equity between supervisor and supervisee?

Video Supervisory Question:

The supervision question that Brad presented during the supervision video was,

> Given the fact that I've taken a fairly traditional cognitive behavioral model and a wellness model and neurotherapy combined with a biofeedback model to address his issues, is there another theoretical approach that I can take that would be fresh for him and uh… maybe hook us into an area that we missed in regard to why he's relapsing?

Theoretical-Specific Supervision and the Case of Brad

When conducting supervision with Brad, one of the first things Lori did was listen to his supervision question. She selected a psychodynamic theory and some Jungian construct because Brad was searching for a new and fresh approach. Lori chose Psychodynamic Supervision and tried to adhere to its tenets throughout the supervisory process. In Psychodynamic Supervision additional emphasis may be on parallel process (Doehrman, 1976). The definition of parallel process is that the dynamic that occurs in the client/therapist relationship is played out in the supervisee/supervisor relationship. As Brad's supervisor, Lori needed to focus on any resistance that Brad and his client had during the session and investigate what resistance he may have toward the supervisor.

Neurocounseling and Its Implications for Homeostatic Plasticity

As many of you know, neurocounseling is a relatively new addition to the counseling world (Russell-Chapin, 2016). A *Counseling Today* journalist had an interview with several of us to discuss the advantages and disadvantages of integrating neuroscience into the counseling curricula. The article was titled "The Birth of the Neurocounselor?" (Montes, 2013). Since that time, neurocounseling has flourished, as so many counselors can see the benefits of bridging the brain to behavior, and understand that many of our mental health concerns, if not all, have brain-related and physiological underpinnings.

Dr. Thomas Ros, a neurofeedback specialist, and colleagues wrote an excellent article (Ros, Baar, Lanius, & Vuilleumier, 2014) on the concept of homeostatic plasticity helping to explain the theory about how and why neurofeedback works, in addition to the behavioral principles of learning. Homeostatic plasticity refers to neuronal capacity of regulating excitability relative to network activity (Turrigiano & Nelson, 2004). This means there is a compensatory adjustment that occurs over time. As our neurons in the brain are striving for homeostasis, physiologically our bodies and brain are striving for homeostasis and allostasis.

Take that a step farther, as our supervisees are learning new skills, supervisors must teach them that change will occur and is healthy, and adaptation and adjustment are occurring and will occur through each supervision session. The brain loves to be challenged, and it actually needs to be challenged for growth to occur. It is the same concept with supervision. Supervisees need to be challenged to grow. There may be growing pains, but adaption will occur. As mentioned in an earlier chapter, a healthy and safe supervisory environment will be the best place to be challenged. There appears to be an intentional and most effective way to challenge supervisees.

Recently Borders, Welfare, Sackett, and Cashwell (2017) conducted research showing that supervisees typically want direct feedback, so supervisors need skills to gain the confidence to share positive, constructive feedback. In other research, the most and least helpful supervision events were studied. This group discovered that the most helpful events in supervision emphasized personal awareness aspects in individual supervision, triadic peer supervision feedback, and learning from others in group supervision (Fickling, Borders, Mobley, & Wester, 2017).

Summary

As stated earlier, theoretical-specific or discipline-specific supervision can be rich with supervision material. The strengths of this approach far outweigh the supervisor's fears of not being competent enough to help the supervisee. The supervisor may need to review counseling theories from the past, and if there is no solid knowledge base, then a referral or consultation may occur. If the supervisor is willing to stretch out of a familiar counseling zone, growth for both the supervisor and supervisee will occur. The supervisor needs to be cognizant, however, of the possible need for additional resources and models to round out the supervision needs.

Remember the construct of homeostatic plasticity. Everything and everyone is constantly striving for growth and adaptability. Regardless of theoretical orientation and theoretical-specific supervision, supervisees need and want to grow. Help them intentionally and kindly.

Chapter Five Final Discussion Questions:

1. Based on Brad's supervision question and case presentation, how was the Psychodynamic Supervision Model a wise choice? Find possible solutions in the chapter text.

_____

_____

_____

_____

2. Think of a supervision moment when you as a supervisor or supervisee were observing a specific theoretical orientation skill. What would be the advantages of focusing on one theoretical orientation in supervision? Disadvantages?

_____

_____

_____

_____

3. What is your opinion about the best manner to offer feedback for the best chance of growth?

_____

_____

_____

_____

References

Bernard, J.M. & Goodyear, R.K. (1998). _Fundamentals of clinical supervision._ Needham Heights, MA: Allyn & Bacon.

Borders, L.D., Welfare, L.E., Sackett, C.R., & Cashwell, C.S. (2017). New supervisors' struggles and successes with corrective feedback. *Counselor Education and Supervision*, 56(3), 208–224. doi:10.1002/ceas.12073

Bowlby, J. (1988). *A secure base: Parent–child attachment and healthy human development*. New York, NY: Basic Books.

Bradley, L.J. & Gould, L.J. (2001). Psychotherapy-based models of counselor supervision. In L.J. Bradley & N. Ladany (Eds.), *Counselor supervision: Principles, process and practice* (3rd ed.). Philadephia: Brunner Routledge.

Carta-Falsa, J. & Anderson, L. (2001). A model of clinical/counseling supervision. *The California Therapist*, 13(2), 47–51.

Corey, G. (2001). *Theory and practice of counseling and psychotherapy* (6th ed.). Pacific Grove, CA: Brooks/Cole.

Doehrman, M. (1976). Parallel processes in supervision and psychotherapy. *Bulletin of the Menninger Clinic*, 40, 3–104.

Dryden, W. (2014). *Rational emotive behavior therapy: Distinctive features* (2nd ed.). New York, NY: Routledge.

Ellis, A. (1989). Thoughts on supervising counselors and therapists. *Psychology: A Journal of Human Behavior*, 26, 3–5.

Fickling, M.J., Borders, L.D., Mobley, K., & Wester, K. (2017). Most and least helpful events in three supervision modalities. *Counselor Education and Supervision*, 56, 289–303. doi:10.1002/ceas.12086

Frawley-O'Dea, M.G. & Sarnat, J.E. (2001). *The supervisory relationship: A contemporary psychodynamic approach*. New York, NY: Guilford Press.

Goldstein, E.G. (2001). *Object relations and self psychology in social work practice*. New York, NY: Simon Schuster.

Hackney, H.L. & Goodyear, R.K. (1984). Carl Rogers' client-centered supervision. In R.F. Levant and J.M. Schlep (Eds.), *Client-centered therapy and the person-centered approach*. New York, NY: Praeger.

Haynes, R., Corey, G., & Moulton, P. (2003). *Clinical supervision in the helping professions: A practical guide*. Pacific Grove, CA: Brooks/Cole.

Holloway, E.L. (1995). *Clinical supervision: A systems approach*. Thousand Oaks, CA: Sage.

Ladany, N., Friedlander, M.L., & Nelson, M.L. (2005). *Critical events in Psychotherapy Supervision: An interpersonal approach*. Washington, DC: American Psychological Association.

Lambers, E. (2000). Supervision in person-centered therapy: Facilitating congruence. In E. Mearns & B. Thorne (Eds.), *Person-centered therapy today: New frontiers in theory and Practice* (pp. 196–211). London: Sage.

Liese, B.S. & Beck, J.S. (1997). Cognitive therapy supervision. In C.E. Watkins Jr. (Ed.), *Handbook of psychotherapy supervision* (pp. 114–133). New York, NY: John Wiley.

Mikulincer, M. & Shaver, P.R. (2007). *Attachment in adulthood: Structure, dynamics and change*. New York, NY: Guilford Press.

Montes, S. (2013). The birth of a neurocounselor? *Counseling Today*, 56, 33–40.

Morgan, M.M. & Sprenkle, D.H. (2007). Toward a common-factors approach to supervision. *Journal of Marital and Family Therapy*, 33(1), 1–17.

Patterson, C.H. (1997). Client-centered supervision. In C.E. Watkins Jr. (Ed.), *Handbook of psychotherapy supervision* (pp. 134–146). New York, NY: John Wiley.

Pistole, M.C. & Fitch, J.C. (2008). Attachment theory in supervision: A critical incident experience. *Counselor Education & Supervision*, 3(47), 193–205.

Prouty, A. (2001). Experiencing feminist family therapy supervision. *Journal of Feminist Family Therapy*, 12, 171–203.

Prouty, A.M., Thomas, V., Johnson, S., & Long, J.K. (2001). Methods of feminist family therapy supervision. *Journal of Marital and Family Therapy*, 27, 85–97.

Rogers, C.R. (1961). *On becoming a person.* Boston: Houghton Mifflin.

Ros, T., Baar, B.J., Lanius, R.A., & Vuilleumier, P. (2014). Tuning pathological brain oscillations with neurofeedback: A systems neuroscience framework. *Frontiers in Neuroscience,* 8(1008), 1–16. doi:10.3389/fnhum.2014.01008

Russell-Chapin, L.A. (2016). Integrating neurocounseling into the counseling profession: An introduction. *Journal of Mental Health Counseling,* 2(38), 93–101. doi:.10.7441/mehc.38.2.01.

Russell-Chapin, L.A. (2007). Supervision: An essential for professional counselor development. In J. Gregoire & C.M. Jungers (Eds.), *The counselor's companion: What every beginning counselor needs to know.* Mahwah, NJ: Lawrence Erlbaum.

Turrigiano, G.G. & Nelson, S.B. (2004). Homeostatic plasticity in the development nervous system. *Nature Reviews Neuroscience,* 5(2), 97–107.

Walsh, J. (2009). *Theories for direct social work practice.* Belmont, CA: Wadsworth/Cengage Learning.

White, M.B. & Russell, C.S. (1995). The essential elements of supervisory systems: A modified Delphi study. *Journal of Marital and Family Therapy,* 21, 33–53.

Woods, P.J., & Ellis, A. (1996). Supervision in rational emotive behavior therapy. *Journal of Rational-Emotive & Cognitive Behavior Therapy,* 14, 135–152.

6

SOCIAL ROLE SUPERVISION MODELS

Overview

Social role supervision models provide the benefit of identifying and emphasizing the varied roles and foci that supervisors need. It is a supervision model that offers structure and interventions for both the supervisee and supervisor. These models also assist the supervisory process by emphasizing the importance of interpersonal communication skills used by the supervisee. The neurocounseling construct for this chapter is understanding the importance of the Default Mode Network (DMN). This brain network is especially critical to clinical supervision when focusing on relationships.

Goals

- Identify the varying roles and foci that supervisees need.
- Understand when these models may be selected.
- Identify fundamentals of the social role supervision models.

Social Role Supervision Models

Social role supervision models tend to describe and organize what supervisors need to do rather than focus on a specific counseling theory (Holloway, 1995). These models acknowledge that the supervisor and supervisee have much wisdom and experience between the two parties from professional role experiences, knowledge base, and conceptualizations about counseling and the supervision process (Bernard & Goodyear, 2004; Casile, Gruber, & Rosenblatt, 2007). Three social role supervision models will be discussed.

Discussion Question #1:

What are the benefits of emphasizing the roles that the supervisor might employ?

_____

_____

_____

_____

Bernard and Goodyear's Discrimination Supervision Model

The most widely known social role model is the Discrimination Supervision Model. It has been extensively researched, and supporters of this type of supervision believe it is an inclusive approach to supervision, as it has its roots in technical eclecticism (Bernard & Goodyear, 1998). One of the main goals of the Discrimination Supervision Model is to focus on the needs of the supervisee by being able to respond flexibly with any needed strategy, technique, and/or guidance.

It is situation specific, and the supervisor emphasizes two primary functions during each supervision session, that of the supervisor's role and focus. There are three roles that a supervisor would take based upon supervisee's needs: teacher, counselor, and consultant. Based on supervisory needs, the supervisor might put on the teacher's hat and role and directly instruct and demonstrate constructs and skills. The supervisor may need to be in the counselor's role to assist the supervisee in locating "blind spots" or becoming aware of, perhaps, some personal countertransference issues. Finally, there may be times during supervision when what is required is a need for the supervisor to bounce back and forth intervention ideas surrounding a client and become the supervisee's colleague and consultant (Russell-Chapin, Sherman, & Ivey, 2016; Russell-Chapin & Ivey, 2004; Russell-Chapin, 2007).

Table 6.1 Areas of Focus

Role Focus	Definition
Process	Examines how you communicate with your client.
Conceptualization	Explores your intentions behind the chosen skill interventions.
Personalization	Identifies mannerisms used to interact with clients such as body language, voice intonation.

Each of these roles of teacher, counselor, and consultant emphasizes three areas of focus for skill-building purposes. These three areas of focus are: process, conceptualization, and personalization. A supervision student recently shared his confusion with these role and foci. My clarifying example came from a hypothetical supervisee unconsciously scooting his chair back when the client talked about the relationship with his mother. The teacher role may be necessary to point out that personalization behavior. Then the counselor hat may need to be worn to explore the why or what of that behavior using a very different and unique skill set. If those insights are addressed, the consultant role could be used to identify possible strategies for change. Within one focus, all three roles could be needed and utilized, or a supervisor may only use one role. Now you may want to study and review the chart for the definition of each focus area.

Basic Tenet

Supervisees benefit from those supervisors who work from multiple theoretical orientations and focus on supervisee's needs by being able to respond flexibly with any needed strategy, technique, and/or guidance based upon the supervisor's role and focus.

When to Use

When the supervisee is unaware of own experience with clients, the Discrimination Model assists in expanding counseling knowledge base.

Supervisor's Roles and Behaviors

- The supervisor responds flexibly with needed role of teacher, counselor, and/or consultant guidance.
- The supervisor selects the necessary focus.

Supervisor's Emphasis and Goals

- Emphasize two primary functions during each supervision session, that of the supervisors' role and focus.
- Three supervisor roles selected based upon supervisee needs are: teacher, counselor, and consultant.
- Each of these roles has three areas of foci for skill-building purposes.
- The three areas of focus are: process, conceptualization, and personalization.

Limitations

There is limited empirical evidence testing the efficacy of the social role models (Holloway, 1992; Morgan & Sprenkle, 2007). This model may not be inclusive enough to meet all of the supervisee's needs.

Discussion Questions #2:

1. How does the Discrimination Supervision Model help the supervisee and supervisor "discriminate" between what roles, foci, and responses are needed?

2. When using the Discrimination Supervision Model, which of the foci would be most helpful to you as a supervisor and supervisee?

3. Which role would be the most difficult for you as a supervisor?

Holloway's Social Role Supervision Model

Holloway (1995) created a similar model to the original Discrimination Model (Bernard, 1979) but added additional depth and complexity to the social role configuration by offering five supervisory functions, five tasks, and four general contextual factors (Morgan & Sprenkle, 2007). Holloway's 5x5 grid creates a process matrix for supervisors to determine the effectiveness of the selected tasks, functions, and methods (Morgan & Sprenkle, 2007).

The five functions and tasks interact with the four factors. The five functions are: (1) monitor and evaluate, (2) instruct and advise, (3) model, (4) consult, and (5) support and share. The functions fall on a continuum of most structure and direction to less structure and more consultation. Lanning and Freeman (1994) added to this model another fundamental function that all supervisors need to address and model. Lanning (1986) believes the function of understanding and practicing professional and ethical behaviors is a must.

Basic Tenet

The Holloway Social Role Supervision Model believes in the importance of roles and foci but adds the additional supervisory functions, tasks, and contextual factors.

When to Use

Use this supervision model when additional structure and evaluation are required to determine the effectiveness of the supervisee and supervisor.

Supervisor's Roles and Behaviors

The supervisor uses the 5x5 process grid to examine the supervisory functions, tasks, and roles.

Supervisor's Emphasis and Goals

The supervisor's main goal is to provide a comprehensive approach for conducting supervision using roles, foci, tasks, functions, and context.

Limitations

The grid format assists in structuring the supervision process, but the grid can also be complex and intimidating to follow.

Discussion Questions #3:

1. How do the additional five functions supplement this social role model?

_____

_____

_____

_____

2. Why might adding the function of professional behaviors be important to the supervisory process?

_____

_____

_____

_____

Hawkins and Shohet's Social Role Supervision Model

Another major social role model of supervision is the six-focused approach of Hawkins and Shohet (2000). The six categories are interwoven into the two systems at work in supervision: the therapy and supervision systems. The six foci are: (1) reflection on the content of the therapy session, (2) exploration of the strategies and interventions the counselor uses, (3) exploration of the therapy process and relationship, (4) focus on the counselor's countertransference, (5) focus on here-and-now process as a mirror or parallel of the there-and-then, and (6) focus on the supervisor's countertransference. These six foci are worked through within the context of counseling and the context of supervision.

Basic Tenet

In the Hawkins and Shohet's Social Role Supervision Model the main tenet emphasizes six foci and two systems.

When to Use

Use this model when there is a belief that countertransference issues on both the supervisee and supervisor exist in counseling and supervision.

Supervisor's Roles and Behaviors

Within the structure of foci and systems, the supervisor is an active director in the supervisory process.

Supervisor's Emphasis and Goals

The major goal is to strategically and comprehensively maneuver through the six foci and the counseling and supervision systems.

Limitations

This approach is comprehensive yet time-consuming.

Discussion Question #4:

1. In this social role supervision model, there are six foci to consider. In your mind which foci might be more essential to the supervisory process? Are they equally important? Explain.

_____

_____

_____

_____

As the reader begins to assimilate all the social role supervision models, again look for the similarities and differences. This is the supervisor's and supervisee's opportunity to develop a unique and individualized model that works for the supervisory team.

Video Supervisory Question:

The supervision question that was offered to Lori assisted her in determining the best supervision model. Here is Jason's question: "Because he's not coming in directly to work with OCD, but he's kind of bridging that gap here, how am I supposed to work to decide whether … thinking and having those thoughts (suicide) that maybe I do, but I don't think I do, or are they two separate identities?"

Supervision and the Case of Jason

Jason's supervision question helped Lori key in on Jason's supervision needs. First Lori selected the foci and role to use to accomplish the needed supervision goal and answer Jason's supervision question. She chose to focus on Jason's basic intervention skills by being in the role of teacher and counselor. Lori tried to actually teach new skills and understand Jason's effect on the client.

The elegance of Discrimination Supervision is that as Lori continues to supervise Jason, the foci and roles would change across sessions and within sessions (Bernard & Goodyear, 1998).

Neurocounseling Implications for Supervision

Offering supervisees opportunities for exploration and reflection builds accountability and independent thinking. Understanding the structure and function of the brain's Default Mode Network (DMN) aids in realizing the importance of introspection, self-awareness, and mind wandering to the overall health of supervisees.

The Default Mode Network serves as a resting state or non-attending, goal-related function in the brain. The DMN houses several regions of the brain: prefrontal cortex, posterior cingulate cortex, the parietal lobes and temporal lobes (Jones, 2017). When a healthy, regulated person is not involved in a specific and goal-driven task, the DMN will be activated. Research has demonstrated that, in fact, often children with ADHD can't activate the DMN when in a resting state (Russell-Chapin et al., 2013). A healthy DMN seems to be essential to understanding self and the world around us. Therefore, time for introspection and reflection is crucial to our overall development.

In a wonderful article on the DMN, Goncalves (2015) wrote about the need for mind wandering in counseling for counselors and clients. All helping professionals have been taught to practice attending and active listening skills. Those micro and macro skills are essential to comprehending the overall picture of the client's concern. Sometimes, though, the moments of feeling lost or mind wandering are the DMN's activation and way of helping us process and better understand the world around us.

The process of clinical supervision is no different. Allow the DMN to activate and reflect on the complex variables surrounding supervision. When wandering occurs as a supervisor or supervisee, please don't think this is a sign of a poor supervisor or supervisee. If both parties agree, ahead of time, to articulate when this process does occur and the DMN becomes activated, then discuss where the thoughts and feelings were headed. This may actually guide and offer direction to the original supervision question.

Summary

Social role models of supervision offer the supervisor and supervisee essential structure to supervision sessions. Having the supervisor select the needed role and foci assists the supervisee in learning new skills, conceptual themes, and unknown factors inhibiting the counseling and supervision process. Better understanding the role of the Default Mode Network may benefit the supervision process.

Chapter Six Final Discussion Questions:

1. Based on Jason's supervision question and his case presentation, how was the supervisor successful in addressing the supervisee's specific needs?

_____

_____

_____

_____

2. What are some of the advantages and disadvantages of selecting the Discrimination Supervision Model for this supervisee?

_____

_____

_____

_____

3. As a supervisor what role and specific focus would you feel comfortable displaying with each of your supervisees?

_____

_____

_____

4. Which roles and specific focus would be difficult for you?

_____

_____

_____

_____

5. When your mind wanders in supervision, what are some of the thoughts and feelings you are experiencing? What do you typically say to yourself when you wander from the process?

_____

_____

_____

_____

References

Bernard, J.M. (1979). Supervisory training: A discrimination model. *Counselor Education and Supervision*, 18, 60–68.

Bernard, J.M. & Goodyear, R.K. (2004). *Fundamentals of clinical supervision* (3rd ed.). Boston: Pearson/Allyn & Bacon.

Bernard, J.M. & Goodyear, R.K. (1998). *Fundamentals of clinical supervision*. Needham Heights, MA: Allyn & Bacon.

Casile, W.J., Gruber, E.A., & Rosenblatt, S.N. (2007). Collaborative supervision for the novice supervisor. In J. Gregorie & C.M. Jungers (Eds.), *The counselor's companion: What every beginning counselor needs to know* (pp. 93–94). Mahwah, NJ: Lawrence Erlbaum.

Goncalves, O.F. (2015). The counselor's wandering mind: Being empathic by default. *Counseling Today*, April, 12–15.

Hawkins, P. & Shohet, R. (2000). *Supervision in the helping professions* (2nd ed.). Philadelphia: Open University Press.

Holloway, E.L. (1995). *Clinical supervision: A systems approach*. Thousand Oaks, CA: Sage.

Holloway, E.L. (1992). Supervision: A way of teaching and learning. In S.D. Brown & R.W. Lent (Eds.), *Handbook of counseling psychology* (2nd ed., pp. 177–214). New York, NY: John Wiley.

Howard, G.S., Nance, D.W., & Myers, P. (1986). Adaptive counseling and therapy: An integrative, eclectic model. *The Counseling Psychologist*, 14, 363–442.

Jones, L. (2017). Anatomy and brain development. In T. Field, L. Jones, & L. Russell-Chapin (Eds.), *Neurocounseling: Brain-based clinical approaches* (pp. 3–24). Alexandria, VA: American Counseling Association.

Lanning, W. (1986). Development of a supervisor emphasis rating form. *Counselor Education and Supervision*, 25, 191–196.

Lanning, W. & Freeman, B. (1994). The supervisor emphasis rating form-revised: Counselor which roles and specific focus would be difficult for you? *Education and Supervision*, 33, 254–304.

Morgan, M.M. & Sprenkle, D.H. (2007). Toward a common-factors approach to supervision. *Journal of Marital and Family Therapy*, 33(1), 1–17.

Russell-Chapin, L.A. (2007). Supervision: An essential for professional counselor development. In J. Gregorie & C.M. Jungers (Eds.), *The counselor's companion: What every beginning counselor needs to know* (pp. 79–80). Mahwah, NJ: Lawrence Erlbaum.

Russell-Chapin, L.A., Sherman, N.E., & Ivey, A.E. (2016). *Your supervised practicum and internship: Field resources for turning theory into practice* (2nd ed.). New York, NY: Routledge.

Russell-Chapin, L.A., Kemmerly, T., Liu, W.C., Zagardo, M.T., Chapin, T., Dailey, D., & Dinh, D. (2013). The effects of neurofeedback in the default mode network: Pilot study results of medicated children with ADHD. *Journal of Neurotherapy*, 17(1), 35–42.

Russell-Chapin, L.A. & Ivey, A.E. (2004). *Your supervised practicum and internship: Field resources for turning theory into practice.* Pacific Grove, CA: Brooks/Cole.

7

INTEGRATED MODELS
OF SUPERVISION

Overview

Integrated models of supervision tend to be atheoretical and use concepts from other counseling theories that are needed by supervisees. There are many ways that a supervisor and supervisee can formulate an integrated theory. Understanding the definition of integration and eclecticism is essential however. In this chapter the integrated model of Microcounseling Supervision offers a standardized approach to supervision offering to the supervisee strengths and areas for improvement. Follow along using the chapter transcription for a demonstration of the integrated Microcounseling Supervision Model. Incorporating the neurocounseling construct of brain activation and active listening skills of both the supervisee and supervisor will be discussed.

Goals

- Understand the tenets behind integrated models of supervision.
- Understand the differences between technical eclecticism and theoretical integration.
- See how Microcounseling Supervision can be used with all supervision models.

Integrated Model of Supervision

Often when helping professionals are asked about their theoretical orientation, many clinicians will state they are eclectic in their views. To assist those who favor eclecticism, integrated models of supervision were designed for those who work from multiple theoretical orientations. Two approaches toward developing an integrated model are technical eclecticism and theoretical integration. Technical eclecticism takes techniques and interventions from many different theoretical orientations and uses them as needed without necessarily believing in a specific orientation. Theoretical integration, on the other hand, blends theoretical constructs and techniques from different theories to create a different and possibly better outcome for clients (Haynes, Corey, & Moulton, 2003; Norcross & Halgin, 1997).

Stoltenberg (2008) suggests there are three broad categories of supervision models: process-based, psychotherapy-based, and competency-based approaches. As discussed in previous chapters, process-based models focus on roles and tasks such as social role models. Psychotherapy-based models emphasize specific counseling disciplines such as psychodynamic, and competency-based models highlight needed skills and best practice behaviors. The Microcounseling Supervision Model discussed in the next section is an example of an integrated and competency-based approach to supervision.

Discussion Question #1:

What could be advantages of conducting supervision using supervision models that are eclectic, integrated, and atheoretical?

_____

_____

_____

_____

Microcounseling Supervision Model

Microcounseling Supervision Model (MSM) falls into the category of integrated and competency-based supervision, and it is our belief that

MSM successfully combines and uses many of the skills from a variety of theories and supervision models by reviewing basic interviewing skills that are used in most theoretical orientations and counseling interviews (Russell-Chapin & Ivey, 2004b; Russell-Chapin, 2007). MSM combines both technical eclecticism and theoretical integration to create a supervision model that almost all counseling theories can use.

The beauty of Microcounseling Supervision is that it teaches the supervisee and supervisor a natural method for reviewing counseling tapes and offering feedback, regardless of theoretical orientation. The MSM is a standardized approach assisting the supervisee in reviewing, offering feedback, teaching, and evaluating microcounseling skills. Lambert and Ogles (1997) described microcounseling skills as an approach that facilitates the general purposes of psychotherapy no matter what the theoretical orientation. The effectiveness of microcounseling skills training has been researched for decades (Miller, Morrill, Uhlemann, 1970; Scisson, 1993). In 1989, Baker and Daniels analyzed 81 studies on microcounseling skills training. Their findings concluded that microcounseling skills training surpassed both the no training and attention-placebo-control comparison. Daniels (2002) has followed microcounseling research for many years and now has identified over 450 data-based studies on the model.

Russell-Chapin and Sherman (2000) found, even with the effectiveness of the microcounseling approach, little consistency in the strategies used to actually measure and evaluate counseling students' skills and videotapes. Russell-Chapin and Sherman stated, "The need for quantifying counselor skills becomes increasingly important as the counseling profession continues to develop and refine standards for counselor competence" (2000, p. 116).

The Counseling Interview Rating Form (CIRF) was designed in response to that very need to accurately and effectively supervise students' counseling videotapes and live supervision sessions (Russell-Chapin & Sherman, 2000). The CIRF has a variety of functions, but it's mostly used as a method of providing positive and corrective feedback for supervisee counseling tapes. For additional information about the construction, reliability, and validity of the CIRF, refer to the Russell-Chapin and Sherman (2000).

A major focus of the Microcounseling Supervision Model provides a vocabulary guide, a framework for constant examination of individual counseling style, and a method for offering feedback (Russell-Chapin & Ivey, 2004a). In beginning skills classes students are encouraged to give others feedback. Usually the comments are very positive, "You were great," or "I liked the way you paraphrased." During supervision, though, more than positive feedback must be given. If constructive feedback is not provided to students during supervision, progress will be stagnant and perhaps nonexistent. This model offers a way for the supervisor and supervisee to learn to give constructive feedback incorporating strengths and areas for improvement by following the format of the Counseling Interview Rating Form (CIRF).

The CIRF is the mechanism used to accomplish this framework, and is an integral part of the MSM. This instrument can be utilized for qualitative and quantitative feedback for counseling interviews.

Discussion Question #2:

Having a standardized approach to supervision has several benefits. Name two benefits that would meet your supervision needs.

_____

_____

_____

_____

The Counseling Interview Rating Form (CIRF)

A major component of Microcounseling Supervision is the Counseling Interview Rating Form. The CIRF was originally developed for a counselor education program, but it has been used in both educational and clinical settings. The CIRF is the structured underpinnings of Microcounseling Supervision, as it provides a format for evaluating the five stages of the counseling interview as described by Ivey, Ivey, and Zalaquett (2018) and the microcounseling skills used in the counseling interview.

The CIRF was created by including the essential listening and influencing skills taught in many helping professional programs. Two categories of skills are included: (a) listening and influencing skills and (b) counseling interview stages. The CIRF is divided into six sections that correspond to the five stages of a counseling interview, plus one additional section on Professionalism. The vocabulary used for the five stages of the interview are: (a) Opening, (b) Exploration, (c) Action, (d) Problem-Solving, and (e) Closing sections. Listed within each section are skills or tasks that are seen in that stage of the interview. The Opening section, for example, includes the specific criteria of greeting, role definition, administrative tasks, and beginning. A blank CIRF is included in Appendix 7.A.

Discussion Question #3:

After looking over the CIRF in Appendix 7.A, jot down any questions about the form. Discuss in your supervisory team. When will the CIRF be most effective for you to use?

_____

_____

_____

_____

Scoring the CIRF

While watching a current videotape or participating in a live counseling supervision session, the CIRF is used to tally the number of times a certain skill is used with frequency marks. If the skill were demonstrated five different times, a frequency tally would be marked each time. Values are assigned after the counseling session to indicate the level of mastery achieved for each skill, and ratings of 1, 2, or 3 for each of the 43 listed skills are given for those skills observed.

Ivey et al. (2018) describe mastery as using the skills with intention with an observable, desired effect on the client. A score of 1 is offered if the counselor was using that skill with little or no effect on the client. A score of 2 says the counselor used the skill with mastery and intention and a score of 3 says the counselor was demonstrating and teaching a new skill or concept to the client. A score of 3 is used sparingly.

The CIRF includes space for comments next to each skill, so any reviewer can make notes or write the counselor's actual statements while viewing the tape. These comments are extremely important to the supervisory session, as these comments can offer the counselor true examples of skills and processes used during the interview. The last page of the CIRF consists of space for providing written feedback on the strengths and areas for improvement. During Microcounseling Supervision, all peer supervisors and the instructor will use the narrative space to provide constructive feedback.

If using the CIRF for quantifying counseling sessions into grades, the total values are tallied, with an A corresponding to 52 points and higher (i.e., at least 90 percent of the total points). This cut-off score requires scoring in the mastery range on all the essential skills denoted by an "X" on the CIRF. Essential skills are those deemed necessary for an effective interview as determined by the CIRF authors and the microcounseling approach to training (Russell-Chapin & Sherman, 2000).

Uses of the CIRF

The CIRF is useful as an evaluative tool for supervisors and peers and for self-evaluation. By using this form as a central foundation to Microcounseling Supervision, you can approach supervision time with less vulnerability as the environment to supervision is not threatening but validating. In addition to an evaluation tool, the CIRF is an excellent teaching tool. Use the CIRF to identify areas and skills frequently used and those skills not being used.

The Three Components of Microcounseling Supervision

The Microcounseling Supervision Model has three major components: (1) Reviewing Skills with Intention, (2) Classifying Skills with Mastery, and (3) Processing Supervisory Needs. Its tenets are based on microcounseling skills first reported by Ivey, Normington, Miller, Morrill, and Haase (1968), and all the skills correspond to the five stages of the counseling interview.

Reviewing Microcounseling Skills with Intention

The first component of the MSM is essential to the efficacy and efficiency of the remaining sections. Supervisees must review each of the basic interviewing skills and understand their intention. Once a supervisee is comfortable and secure with defining and reviewing the microcounseling skills, then the supervisor can assist the supervisee in rapidly entering into the second phase. It is critical that initially the supervisee takes the needed time to ensure that each individual skill definition along with the underlying intention of that skill is understood. Intention is defined as choosing the best potential response from among the many possible options.

In the first MSM stage, the supervisee is not looking for the "right" solution and skill, but is selecting responses to adapt individual counseling style to meet the differing needs and culture of clients (Ivey et al., 2018). With intentionality, supervisees can anticipate specific interviewing results if certain skills are used! For example, if a supervisee wants a client to continue expressing emotions, a basic reflection of feeling would be a wise skill to choose. A client laments, "Today was my little boy's first day of Kindergarten!" The counselor's reflection of feeling is, "There must be many differing emotions going on inside. You could be sad, lonely, scared yet excited!" Review the first step of Microcounseling Supervision by practicing, defining, and reviewing all the microcounseling skills. A glossary of the 43 microcounseling skills with their intentionality is provided in Appendix 7.B.

Discussion Question #4:

Review the glossary of 43 microcounseling skills. Which of those skills need additional clarification? Discuss with your supervisory team.

_____

_____

_____

_____

Classifying Skills with Mastery

The second stage of the MSM is Classifying Counseling Skills with Mastery. One of the easiest methods to begin the second stage is to have examples of someone else demonstrating the microcounseling skills and their uses. When your supervisee is comfortable, allow them to watch a videotape of their own and classify the skills observed using the CIRF. The two of you could share your scores and classifications. Look for the areas of agreement and those areas that are missing.

Summarizing and Processing Supervisory Needs

The final stage of the MSM begins by summarizing and processing the demonstrated skills on the CIRF, as well as other important dimensions of the session. Using the CIRF, begin summarizing skill usage with frequency tallies. Go through the transcript again and use a frequency tally for each of the counseling responses observed. At the end of the session, or during each response, see which of the responses represent basic mastery and active mastery. Remember basic mastery is defined as being able to demonstrate the skill during the interview, and active mastery shows the supervisee producing specific and intentional results from the chosen counseling skill.

The final step is to compare the reader's rating with the authors'. In a regular classroom or a supervision session this final step will be discussing supervisee ratings with classmates and supervisors. Once the CIRF has been tallied by the members of the supervisory team, the narrative process for Microcounseling Supervision can begin. The student counselor will present the interview video and case presentation ahead of time and has been asked to formulate needed supervisory questions and concerns. These issues are addressed as a team in a round-robin fashion going over supervisory concerns, strengths, and areas for improvement. The very last question asked would be, "What did you learn in supervision today that will assist you in more effectively working with this client?" Many of these comments may come from the Strengths and Areas for Improvement sections of the CIRF. The comments on these sections will help the supervisee immensely to progress forward (Russell-Chapin & Ivey, 2004a).

Basic Tenet

Supervisees benefit from a standardized, atheoretical approach assisting them in reviewing, offering feedback, and evaluating micro and macro-counseling skills and the counseling interview.

When to Use

When essential microskills are not effectively utilized, selecting the Microcounseling Supervision Model is suggested.

Supervisor's Roles and Behaviors

- Use the Counselor Interview Rating Form (CIRF) as a mechanism for creating a reciprocal supervision process for offering constructive feedback.
- Choose from the three MSM components based upon supervisee's needs: Reviewing Skills with Intention; Classifying Skills with Mastery; and Processing Supervisory Needs.

Supervisor's Emphasis and Goals

- Assist the supervisee with clarifying and defining all micro and macrocounseling skills.
- Identify and classify observed skills with intention using the CIRF.
- Process the strengths and liabilities of the counseling session answering the supervisory question.

Limitations

The major limitation is that MSM is best utilized when there is a videotape or digital tape of a counseling session. In some settings obtaining a recording of a counseling session does not easily occur.

Video Supervisory Questions:

This supervisee's question was two-fold: "How can I engage him better in counseling and how can I reach Lawrence so he can be more comfortable with me?"

The Supervision Case of Andrea

Andrea asked several supervision questions. After watching her videotape, it seemed she was missing several basic skills, so the integrated Microcounseling Supervision Model made sense to use.

The cardinal rule of any integrative supervision is to customize supervision to meet the needs of the individual supervisee. In other words, "the 'how' of supervision should parallel the 'what' of supervision" (Norcross and Halgin, 1997, p. 210). Lori chose to demonstrate with Andrea how and what could be accomplished by answering her supervision questions.

Neurocounseling and Its Implications for Supervision and Active Listening Skills

In our early counselor training, many of us practiced intentional micro and macrocounseling skills. The idea was that if counselors intentionally selected a particular skill, then we were increasing the odds of obtaining more efficacious answers from our clients. For example, if a closed question is intentionally asked, then the likelihood of a client giving a finite answer is expected. This is true for the supervisory session as well.

From brain scans and research, we know that when the supervisor/counselor practices attending skills creating positive regard the ventral striatum becomes active in both the supervisor/counselor and the supervisee (Ivey et al., 2018). The ventral striatum is often responsible for reward, some decision making, and motivation.

Research has also demonstrated that when summarizations are intentionally selected the Default Mode Network (DMN) is activated. The DMN consists of a large and major brain network and hubs consisting of the posterior cingulate cortex, medial prefrontal cortex, and angular gyrus. It may assist with the Theory of the Mind (TOM) and helps with understanding the world around us. It is the DMN that acts as a resting state and allows us to reflect. It also helps with social working memory (Carter, 2014). How powerful is activating this network in supervision? Better understanding how our counseling skills impact others is essential to counseling success.

The final example is the use of immediacy. Staying in the "here and now" with our supervisees and clients also teaches us to practice using the entire brain networks from the prefrontal cortex and executive functioning to the limbic system and the hypothalamic, pituitary, adrenal (HPA) hormones to the amygdala and memory in the hippocampus.

This list can go on and on, and going on is warranted, but more importantly is the knowledge that what supervisors/counselors do, not only changes the brain and behaviors of both the supervisee and supervisor, but with continued practice neuroplasticity and neurogenesis are occurring in both the supervisor and supervisee! This activation can be seen using fMRIs.

Summary

Observing interview tapes and analyzing case presentations are essential to the growth of novice helping professionals. There are other integrative and/or competency-based supervision models that can be used to do just that, however the Microcounseling Supervision Model (MSM) can be a supervisory method for assisting supervisors and supervisees in naturally strengthening intentional micro and macrocounseling skills. MSM can be used to assist in building a foundation necessary for effective counseling and developmental growth. It provides building blocks for better understanding of basic attending behaviors and influencing skills through the three stages of the MSM: identification, classification, and processing of counseling skills.

The Counseling Interview Rating Form assists in developing a system for reciprocal supervision where supervisees, colleagues, and instructor can offer constructive feedback. This begins a "magic dance" of supervision where an easy and dynamic flow can encourage supervisees to be receptive to new ideas and interventions. The CIRF not only reviews and teaches how to classify specific skills and behaviors but how to evaluate their intention as well. Finally the CIRF assists in examining whether the goals of each interview stage are being achieved. If supervisors and supervisees practice using the MSM and the CIRF, the natural flow of the Microcounseling Supervision will be experienced.

Those same counseling skills being practiced from a supervisory and/or counseling perspective offer a neurocounseling application of building neuronal plasticity and activating very specific portions of the brain. Being intentional now offers an even deeper physiological meaning.

Chapter Seven Final Discussion Questions:

1. Based on Andrea's supervision questions and her case presentation, how was the Microcounseling Supervision Model the best model selection? Why was it chosen as the best fit model?

_____

_____

_____

_____

2. Of the three MSM components (Reviewing Skills with Intention, Classifying Skills with Mastery, and Summarizing and Processing Supervisory Needs), which component currently helps you understand your supervision concerns?

_____

_____

_____

_____

3. Imagine yourself as a supervisee and supervisor using the Microcounseling Supervision Model. What would be the advantages and disadvantages for you in either role?

_____

_____

_____

_____

4. How does intentionally selecting a micro and/or macrocounseling skill build new neuronal pathways and what portions of the brain are activated with specific skills?

_____

_____

_____

_____

References

Baker, S.B. & Daniels, T. (1989). Integrating research on the microcounseling program: A meta-analysis. *Journal of Counseling Psychology*, 36, 213–22.

Carter, R. (2014). *The human brain book: An illustrated guide to its structure, function and disorders*. New York, NY: DK Publishing.

Daniels, T. (2002). Microcounseling research: What over 450 data-based studies reveal. In A. Ivey, M. Ivey, & R. Marx (Eds.), *Leader guide to intentional interviewing and counseling*. Pacific Grove, CA: Brooks/Cole.

Haynes, R., Corey, G., & Moulton, P. (2003). *Clinical supervision in the helping professions: A practical guide*. Pacific Grove, CA: Brooks/Cole.

Ivey, A.E., Ivey, M.B., & Zalaquett, C.P. (2018). *Intentional interviewing and counseling: Facilitating client development in a multicultural world* (9th ed.). Pacific Grove, CA: Brooks/Cole.

Ivey, A.E., Normington, C.J., Miller, C., Morrill, W., & Haase, R. (1968). Microcounseling and attending behavior: An approach to prepracticum counselor training. *Journal of Counseling Psychology*, 15(5), 1–12.

Lambert, M.J. & Ogles, B.M. (1997). The effectiveness of psychotherapy supervision. In C.E. Watkins Jr. (Ed.), *The handbook of psychotherapy supervision* (pp. 421–446). New York, NY: Wiley.

Miller, C., Morrill, W., & Uhlemann, M. (1970). An experimental study of pre-practicum training in communicating test results. *Counselor Education and Supervision*, 9, 171–177.

Norcross, J.C. & Halgin, R.P. (1997). Integrative approaches to psychotherapy supervision. In C.E. Watkins Jr. (Ed.), *Handbook of psychotherapy integration* (pp. 203–222). New York, NY: Basic Books.

Russell-Chapin, L.A. (2007). Supervision: An essential for professional counselor development. In J. Gregorie & C.M. Jungers (Eds.), *The counselor's companion: What every beginning counselor needs to know* (pp. 79–80). Mahwah, NJ: Lawrence Erlbaum.

Russell-Chapin, L. & Ivey, A. (2004a). Microcounselling supervision model: An innovative approach to supervision. *Canadian Journal for Counselling*, 7(3), 165–176.

Russell-Chapin, L. & Ivey, A. (2004b). *Your supervised practicum and internship: Field resources for turning theory into practice*. Pacific Grove, CA: Brooks/Cole.

Russell-Chapin, L.A. & Sherman, N.E. (2000). The counseling interview rating form: A teaching and evaluation tool for counselor education, *British Journal of Guidance and Counseling*, 28(1), 115–124.

Scisson, E.H. (1993). *Counseling for results: Principles and practices of helping professions*. Pacific Grove, CA: Brooks/Cole.

Stoltenberg, C.D. (2008). Supervision. In F.T.L. Leong (Ed.), *Encyclopedia of Counseling: Volume One: Changes and challenges for counseling in the 21st century*. Thousand Oaks, CA: Sage.

APPENDIX 7.A

COUNSELING INTERVIEW RATING FORM

Counselor: _____   Date: _____

Observer: _____   Tape #: _____

Observer: _____   Audio or Video;   (please circle)

Supervisor: _____   Session #: _____

For each of the following specific criteria demonstrated, make a frequency marking every time the skill is demonstrated. Then assign points for consistent skill mastery using the ratings scales below. List any observations, comments, strengths and weaknesses in the space provided. Providing actual counselor phrases is helpful when offering feedback.

Ivey Mastery Ratings

3 Teach the skill to clients (teaching mastery only)

2 Use the skill with specific impact on client (active mastery)

1 Use and/or identify the counseling skill (basic mastery)

Each skill marked by an X should be seen consistently on every tape.

To receive an A on a tape at least 52–58 points must be earned.

To receive a B on a tape at least 46–51 points must be earned.

To receive a C on a tape at least 41–45 points must be earned.

Specific	Frequency	Comments	Skill Mastery Rating
A. Opening/Developing Rapport			
X 1. Greeting			
2. Role Definition/ Expectation			
3. Administrative Tasks			
X 4. Beginning			
B. Exploring Phase/Defining the Problem Micro Skills			
1. Empathy/ Rapport			
2. Respect			
X 3. Nonverbal Matching			
X 4. Minimal Encourager			
X 5. Paraphrasing			
X 6. Pacing/Leading			
X 7. Verbal Tracking			
X 8. Reflect Feeling			
X 9. Reflect Meaning			
X 10. Clarifications			
X 11. Open-ended Questions			
X 12. Summarization			
X 13. Behavioral Description			

X 14. Appropriate Closed Question			
X 15. Perception Check			
X 16. Silence			
X 17. Focusing			
X 18. Feedback			
C. Problem Solving/Defining Skills			
X 1. Definition of Goals			
X 2. Exploration/ Understanding of concerns			
X 3. Development/ Evaluation of Alternatives			
4. Implement Alternative			
5. Special Techniques			
6. Process Counseling			
D. Action Phase/Confronting Incongruities			
1. Immediacy			
2. Self-Disclosure			
3. Confrontation			
4. Directives			
5. Logical Consequences			
6. Interpretation			

E. Closing/Generalization			
X 1. Summarization of Content/Feeling			
X 2. Review of Plan			
3. Rescheduling			
4. Termination of Session			
X 5. Evaluation of Session			
X 6. Follow-up			
F. Professionalism			
1. Developmental Level Match			
2. Ethics			
3. Professional (punctual, attire, etc.)			
G. Strengths:			
H. Areas for Improvement:			

APPENDIX 7.B

GLOSSARY OF CIRF SKILLS

Opening/Developing Rapport Skills

Definition	Intention
Greeting: A simple acknowledgment to the client	Build rapport
Role Definition/Expectation: Description of the counselor roles and intention of counseling; Confidentiality and its limit.	Provide structure
Administrative Tasks: Procedures necessary for counseling such as Client Rights; Payment; Scheduling and Intake Forms	Clarify procedures
Beginning: An open-ended question demonstrating to the client the interview is starting such as "What do you want to work on today?"	Offer an expansive method of beginning the interview

Exploration Phase/Defining the Problem Micro Skills

Definition	Intention
Empathy/Rapport: Behaviors and attitudes indicating understanding and active listening	Encourage the client to continue
Respect: Offering genuine acknowledgment of client's concerns	Build rapport
Nonverbal Matching: Using body gestures and positions to mirror the client's	Build rapport and acceptance
Minimal Encourager: An occasional word or "uh, uh" encouraging the client to continue	Encourage the client to continue

Paraphrasing: Actively rephrasing in the counselor's own words and perceptions what the client has stated such as "Your mother died recently and you miss her."	Create understanding of client's words
Pacing/Leading: Allowing the client to direct the interview flow by counselor matching of words and verbal intonation; Counselor directing when interview flow needs transition	Encourages comfort, discourages resistance
Verbal Tracking: Consistent following of client's verbal direction and themes	Create continuity from client's content
Reflect Feeling: Paraphrase the client's feelings such as "How sad that must be."	Increases understanding of client's feelings
Reflect Meaning: Paraphrasing the client's deeper level of experience such as "Death can be an ending and perhaps a beginning."	Increases wider perspective
Clarifications: Eliminating confusion of terms by seeking clearer understanding of client's words	Eliminates confusion of terms
Openended Questions: Asking global questions for the purpose of receiving maximum or infinite amount of information such as "What do you miss the most about your mother?"	Receives maximum or infinite amount of information
Summarization: Paraphrasing a cluster of themes or topics during the interview providing transition and/or closure	Provides for transition and/or closure
Behavioral Description: Informing the client of what you observe of a behavior or mannerism; "When we began talking about sister and mother's relationship, I noticed your eyes teared up and you moved your chair away from me."	Eliminates assumptions about behaviors and assists in client awareness
Appropriate Closed Question: An intentional question used to obtain a finite amount of information such as "How old were you when your mother died?"	Gains finite amounts of information
Perception Check: A periodic moment to ask the client if your perceptions or ideas about the concern are accurate; "Is that accurate concerning your sister and mother's relationship?"	Check counselor's perception and accuracy
Silence: Allowing purposeful, quiet reflection during the interview	Allows for purposeful, quiet reflection during the interview
Focusing: Consistent and intentional selection of topic, construct, and/or direction in the session	Aids in direction of the session
Feedback: Offering information to the client concerning attitude and behavior such as "Last week you came here with crumpled clothes, but today you have washed your hair and clothes."	Provides awareness about behaviors, thoughts, and feelings

ProblemSolving Skills/Defining Skills

Definition	Intention
Definition of Goals: Statements stipulating directions, outcomes and goals of the client	Stipulates directions for counseling
Exploration/Understanding of Concerns: Using needed micro skills to discover the nature of the concern	Collects essential information about client's concern
Development/Evaluation of Alternatives: Assisting the client in creating a myriad of options for problem solution; assessing the potential and possibilities surrounding each option	Assesses the potential and possibilities surrounding each option
Implement Alternative: Actively planning and articulating necessary steps for placing option into reality	Assists in putting ideas into action
Special Techniques: Any counseling intervention used to assist the client in deeper understanding of the concern such as imagery or an Empty Chair	Provides for the needs of individual clients
Process Counseling: Helping the client understand special themes and dynamics involved in the problem such as loss and fear	Allows for deeper understanding of client issues

Action Phase/Confronting Incongruities

Definition	Intention
Immediacy: Stopping the interview and immediately seeking clarification about a dynamic or observation in the client or between the counselor and client; "You stopped talking after your Dad was mentioned. What is happening right now?"	Keeps the sessions in the here and now
Self-Disclosure: Offering relevant, helpful, and appropriate information about the counselor for the purpose of client assistance; "When my father died, I was 21 years old. My compass was gone, and I was lost."	Assists the client in universality of life
Confrontation: Pointing out client discrepancies between words, behaviors, thoughts	Helps the client to become aware of thoughts and actions
Directives: An influencing statement specifying an action or thought for the client to take; "The next time you visit your Mother's grave, I suggest you write a poem expressing your fears and loneliness."	Offers needed structure for differing developmental client needs; shows acceptance
Logical Consequences: Explain the results/consequences of the client's actions and solutions; the consequences can be natural or logical	Points out results of client decisions
Interpretation: Presenting a new frame of reference on the client's concern possibly through different theoretical orientations; "It may be that the death of your mother forces you to be alone with yourself and your own fears."	Presents a new frame of reference on the client's concern

Closing/Generalization

Definition	Intention
Summarization of Content/Feeling: Closing the session by tying together themes involving subject matter and emotions	Ties together the counseling themes
Review of Plan: Organizing the desired outcome into a plan and reviewing it with the client	Reminds the client of previously discussed ideas
Rescheduling: Arranging for another session if needed	Provides additional counseling opportunities
Termination of Session: Offering appropriate generalizations from counseling to the client's outside world when goals have been achieved	Brings counseling outcomes to the real world
Evaluation of Session: Asking the client to reflect on the essentials of each interview; "What will you take from today's session that will assist you between now and our next meeting?"	Provides tangible counseling outcomes for the client and counselor
Professionalism: Making appropriate professional decisions following unwritten and written organizational mores and guidelines	Adds respect to counselor and client

Professionalism

Definition	Intention
Developmental Level Match: Assessing the client's developmental level and selecting counseling interventions accordingly	Creates intentional responses corresponding to client needs
Ethics: Following a set of ethical guidelines provided by a professional organization; Making appropriate ethical decisions	Assists in remaining prudent in decision-making process

8
INTERPERSONAL
PROCESS RECALL

Overview

Many supervision sessions require digital recordings of counseling interviews or conducting counseling sessions in an actual live observation setting. Interpersonal Process Recall (IPR) developed by Norm Kagan is a widely used approach that is utilized by many supervisors (Haynes, Corey, & Moulton, 2003). This supervision approach allows supervisees to safely analyze their thoughts and feelings about the counseling interview.

Goals

- Discover methods for using IPR with videotapes, live supervision, or after the counseling session.
- Understand the types of questions that can be utilized with IPR.

Interpersonal Process Recall

Borders and Leddick (1998) conducted a national survey of counselor educators and found IPR to be one of two distinct methods used during supervision courses. The reason this may be true is IPR creates a supervision environment where supervisees can safely analyze their communication styles and strategies. Kagan believed that most people act diplomatically and often do not say what they mean or feel. In supervision, then the supervisor encourages the supervisee to reflect and interpret the experience in the counseling session (Kagan, 1976, 1980).

Historically the Interpersonal Process Recall training model began using the psychoanalytic modeling approach of counselors-in-training observing a master counselor conduct counseling interviews. After the session the expert counselor would express his/her feelings, thoughts, and intentional behaviors. The student would then mimic the same skills and process his/her feelings, thoughts, and intentional behaviors (Baker, Daniels, & Greeley, 1990; Crews et al., 2005). This was the beginning of the IPR approach to supervision.

The best way to conduct IPR Supervision is to view a videotape of a counseling session and simply stop the tape at any time to discuss essential personal and/or counseling issues. In this manner supervisees have the opportunity to increase self-awareness and process the relationship dynamics with the client and the supervisor (Haynes, Corey, & Moulton, 2003). The rules of IPR suggest that both the supervisee and supervisor may stop the tape at any given time. The one who stops the interview is the one who speaks first. If the supervisee speaks first, then it is up to the supervisor to give the supervisee enough time and space to reflect options and possibilities (Bernard & Goodyear, 1992).

Discussion Question #1:

What do you foresee as the possible IPR benefits to a supervisee?

Often supervisees will express appreciation during supervision for the immediate and timely feedback. There seems to be a better comprehension of the skills and feedback when visually stopping the videotape and discussing intentional feeling, thoughts, and behaviors. It was the work of Norm Kagan and Allen Ivey that inspired the development of the Microcounseling Supervision Model. Using the Counselor Interview Rating Form (CIRF) while videotaping is just another extension of Kagan's work.

Discussion Questions #2:

1. What type of feedback do you want as a supervisee?

2. What type of feedback do you want as a supervisor?

3. How do you best receive feedback? Directly? Gently? Is it best received when you ask for it? Describe.

IPR Leads and Questions

Kagan called the good supervisor an "inquirer." Study the following list to see the questions and leads that could be asked while using the Interpersonal Process Recall method (Bernard & Goodyear, 1992, p. 102).

Leads That Inspire Affective Exploration
- Did you want to express that feeling at any time?
- What were your thoughts, feelings, and reactions?
- What did you do about that feeling you had?
- What do those feelings mean to you?

Leads That Check Out Unstated Agendas
- If you had more time, where would you have liked to have gone?
- What would you have liked to have said to her or him at this point?
- What had that meant to you?
- What's happening here?

Leads That Encourage Cognitive Examination
- Did the equipment affect you in any way?
- What would you like to have said at this point?
- What thoughts were you having about the other person at that time?
- How do you think the client was seeing you at this point?

Leads That Get at Images
- Were there any pictures, images, or memories flashing through your mind then?
- How do you imagine the client was reacting to you?
- Had you any ideas about what you wanted to do with that?
- Where had that put you in the past?

Leads That Explore Mutual Perceptions between Client and Counselor
- What messages do you think she or he was trying to give you?
- How do you think he or she felt about talking with you at this point?
- Do you think your description of the moment would correspond with your client's description?
- Was she or he giving you any clues as to how she or he was feeling?

Leads That Help Search out Expectations
- Were you expecting anything from your client at that point?
- Did you sense that the client had any expectations of you at that point?
- What was it like for you in your role as counselor?
- What message did you want to give the client? What prevented you from doing so?

Discussion Question #3:

Which of the above inquiry categories would be easiest and most effective for you to ask? Might your selection have something to do with your own personality?

_____

_____

_____

_____

_____

Basic Tenet

Supervisees need an environment where they can safely analyze their communication styles and strategies.

When to Use

If a supervisee seems to be stuck in the counseling interview, this method allows for safe, immediate feedback and a chance to reflect on the counseling experience.

Supervisor's Roles and Behaviors

Stop the videotape at any time to discuss essential personal and/or counseling issues. If a videotape is not available, lead the supervision session with needed questions.

Supervisor's Emphasis and Goals

The main goal is to stop a counseling videotape or supervisory session and use the skill of immediacy to gently discover counseling blocks, styles, and experiences.

Limitations

- This supervision approach is best used with video or digital recordings, so the supervisor can start and stop the interview when processing is required. However a variation of IPR can be used without recordings by asking the supervisee to recall how he/she felt at that moment.
- This model may not be comprehensive enough alone to meet all the supervisee's needs.

Video Supervisory Question:

This supervisory question suggests that the supervisee needs to take the time to reflect on personal clinical skills and attitudes. The supervision question from Beth is: "How do I address this feeling of loss with her when so much of our time is spent focusing on her behaviors?"

Supervision and the Case of Beth

As Lori listened to Beth's supervision question, it was clear that Beth had the needed counseling skills. However she was seeking supervision to help her with her confidence levels. Using Interpersonal Process Recall (IPR) seemed like a natural supervision approach to use with Beth. The first modeling strategy was to build rapport with Beth until she was comfortable enough to self-disclose. Beth easily talked about her job and history at the high school. Lori then moved into IPR by asking Beth targeted questions.

Neurocounseling Implications for IPR and Negative Bias

Interpersonal Process Recall is a supervisory approach that provides a safe environment for supervisees to analyze possible reasons, unconscious and perhaps conscious, for certain counseling behaviors. Neurocounseling offers another potential physiological reason for some of the supervisee/counselor behaviors by defining the evolution of negative bias. Hanson (2016) suggests that humans are hardwired to know what is life-threatening. If we see a tiger chasing us, we will remember that tiger or any tiger, and remember to run! We remember negative events in our life much more and more readily than our positive events. Therefore supervisors must spend at least 20–30 seconds discussing positive aspects of the supervisory session before that message has any chance of getting into the brain. Supervisors must practice the rule of saying what you are going to say; say it again, and then ask the supervisee what did I just say! If you offer any constructive feedback, it only needs to be said one time because of negative bias. In order to have positive bias, the observation must be stated many times. IPR offers this opportunity in an easy and safe environment. Remember we already discussed the polyvagal theory earlier in Chapter Four. When a supervisee feels safety, the entire body relaxes and can even hear the constructive feedback easier without threat. The parasympathetic nervous system is engaged allowing for constructive feedback to be heard and implemented.

Chapter Eight Final Discussion Questions:

1. Was IPR a good model to fit the supervision question? How was this supervision session successful in answering the question?

_____

_____

_____

_____

2. If you could use the IPR supervision method of viewing videotaped sessions, what would the benefits be of this supervision model?

_____

_____

_____

_____

3. Select three IPR questions from the list in this chapter, imagine where the discussion may develop.

_____

_____

_____

_____

4. Explain the concept of negative bias. How can a supervisor practice offsetting this construct in a supervisory session?

_____

_____

_____

_____

References

Baker, S.B., Daniels, T.G., & Greeley, A.T. (1990). Systemic training of graduate-level counselors: Narrative and meta-analytic reviews of three major programs. *The Counseling Psychologist*, 18, 355–421.

Bernard, J.M. & Goodyear, R.K. (1992). *Fundamentals of clinical supervision*. Needham Heights, MA: Allyn & Bacon.

Borders, L.D. & Leddick, G.R. (1998). A nationwide survey of supervisory training. *Counselor Education and Supervision Journal*, 27(3), 271–283.

Crews, J., Smith, M.R., Smaby, M.H., Maddux, C.D., Torres-Rivera, E., Casey, J., & Urbani, S. (2005). Self-monitoring and counseling skills: Skills-based versus interpersonal process recall training. *Journal of Counseling and Development*, 83(1), 78–85.

Hanson, R. (2016). Hardwiring happiness: The new brain science for contentment, calm and confidence. New York, NY: Crown Publishing.

Haynes, R., Corey, G., & Moulton, P. (2003). *Clinical supervision in the helping profession: A practical guide*. Pacific Grove, CA: Brooks/Cole.

Kagan, N. (1976). *Influencing human interaction*. Mason, MI: Mason Media.

Kagan, N. (1980). Influencing human interaction – eighteen years with IPR. In A.K. Hess (Ed.), *Psychotherapy supervision: Theory, research and practice* (pp. 262–286). New York, NY: Wiley.

9
BENEFITS OF GROUP
SUPERVISION

Overview

In the last 15 years, the increased demand for counseling services and the economic impact of limited third-party reimbursement have resulted in extraordinary demands on individual practitioners. Ever-increasing overhead costs, lengthening work schedules, and professional isolation have caused them to consider the many benefits of the group practice model. Along the way, many practitioners also realized the advantages of consolidating their supervisory needs, therefore interest in group supervision experienced a remarkable resurgence.

This chapter will outline the purpose and the many advantages of group supervision, and some of the limitations of this model. It will also outline a procedure that can be readily applied to many mental health settings. Special attention will be given to the facilitator's role and the many clinical issues that group supervision can address. Finally, the chapter will close with a brief review of some related but vitally important topics that will explore some of the following questions: Should participation in group supervision be voluntary or mandatory? Should mental health professionals be charged for supervision? What kind of documentation will the facilitator need to keep? How can a group handle an issue involving an impaired therapist? How does group supervision change in various work settings? When is group supervision just not enough?

The neurocounseling integration of the function of the parietal lobes into group supervision will be discussed.

Goals

- Identify the advantages and limitations of group supervision.
- Offer a basic procedure for group supervision.
- Observe a demonstration of group supervision of a supervisor becoming the supervisee.

Group Supervision

The primary purpose of group supervision is to provide a rich opportunity for reflection, clinical input, continued professional education and skill enhancement, professional wellness, collegial support, and staff development. Imagine the vast array of experience and knowledge in a room filled with a multidisciplinary team of freshly trained and well-seasoned professional counselors, social workers, psychologists, and psychiatrists. Imagine even further, the value in the participation of many allied professionals including but not limited to: nurses, nutritionists, rehabilitation specialists, and vocational experts. The diversity of professional perspective and theoretical orientation alone can't help but yield a superior advantage in the formulation of an effective treatment plan. In addition, the mere multiplicity of various eyes and ears on a clinical problem would certainly extend any therapist's depth of understanding and potential options toward the client's successful treatment. Current research on group supervision will challenge old ideas about supervision and keep the profession growing (Russell-Chapin & Ivey, 2004). Research results have great implications for future direction in supervision. Ray and Altekruse (2000) conducted group supervision research and found that group supervision is not only complementary to individual supervision but actually may be exchanged for individual supervision. In a summary of the best practices in clinical supervision, an Association for Counselor Education and Supervision (ACES, 2011) task force outlined several important considerations for group supervision that were incorporated into Borders et al.'s (2014) publication, "Best Practices in Clinical Supervision." These included: to be intentional about structure and goals, to differentiate and inform supervisees of the complementary nature of individual, triadic, and group supervision, to establish session ground rules, employ group facilitation skills, foster meaningful feedback, balance member participation, encourage increasing member autonomy and leadership, and assist in generalization of learning toward client benefit.

The primary mechanism for self-awareness, growth, and learning in effective supervision is reflection or the ability to evaluate one's experiences to develop insight and critical thinking (Heller & Gilkerson, 2009; Orchowski, Evangelista, & Probst, 2010). Reflection can be encouraged in many ways. Journaling can help integrate new experience and insight. The use of brainstorming strategies in group supervision can communicate openness to new ideas. Search for themes or a call for alternate hypotheses can validate multiple perspectives. Even supervisor modeling of reflection by sharing their own difficult professional experiences can create a safer environment for discussion of everyone's therapeutic dilemmas, clinical blind spots, or emotional reactions to difficult cases.

In addition to these structural and process elements, group supervision is also effective in providing continued professional education, skill development, and therapist wellness. No single professional can reasonably keep up with the burgeoning literature or specialty certifications that a group of professionals possess. It's not uncommon in group supervision for a participating therapist to share a helpful article, explain an alternate theoretical perspective, or even demonstrate a newly learned therapeutic skill. This helps the young therapist add to their therapeutic tool kit and the mature therapist to refresh their skills as they pass their knowledge on to others. Even more advantageous is the opportunity for the group supervision format to promote members' overall wellness. In line with the Council for Accreditation of Counseling and Related Educational Programs's (CACREP, 2015) directive to attend to the personal wellness of counselors-in-training (CITs) and professional counselors, Wolf, Thompson, Thompson, and Smith-Adock (2014) demonstrated the positive impact of wellness workshops on CITs' self-awareness, connection to spirituality, and ability to maintain balance. Applying this to provider self-care, where emotionally demanding work and risk of burnout are high, the group supervision format can also incorporate a wellness paradigm, by encouraging members to support the engagement of healthy behavior and attend to their own personal wellness (Hollingsworth, 2018).

Perhaps more subtle, but none-the-less important, is the collegial support and camaraderie that group supervision can create among its participants. It is not easy to be vulnerable with your peers, to ask for help, or to admit that you are struggling with a case. It's also not easy to risk sharing your ideas, feelings, intuition, and even special expertise with a colleague. What if you embarrass yourself by displaying your inadequacy? What if your input is ignored or, even worse, argued against by another group member? What if the dual roles of colleague and supervisor create roadblocks to open discussion and reflection? There is emotional risk in group supervision but there is even more potential reward when you find direction with a perplexing problem or receive sincere gratitude from an appreciative colleague. Research on the potential problems with dual roles and disclosure has found that supervisor disclosure explains supervisee disclosure (Kreider, 2014). In other words, the more a supervisor is open, self-disclosing, and receptive to feedback, the more the supervisee will respond in-kind. Well-facilitated group supervision has an enormous potential for building collegial support and enhancing overall group moral.

Finally, group supervision offers the opportunity for meaningful staff development. We all started out as rookies with lots of book knowledge and precious little professional experience. While we may have felt we were well prepared to help our clients, we soon found out that sitting face to face with a complex problem we've never seen before or being humbled by a seemingly impossible therapeutic impasse, is altogether another matter. Group supervision affords us the opportunity to benefit from all the experience of each professional in the group. Chances are someone has been right where we are, struggled with the same problem, and found a way through it. Someday, we, too, will be in that experienced position, and then we'll pass our knowledge and experience on to another therapeutic "rookie." Thus group supervision is an invaluable source for staff development.

Discussion Question #1:

What are your thoughts about the importance of group supervision to the counseling profession?

_____

_____

_____

_____

_____

Advantages

The most obvious advantage of group supervision is that it maximizes the resources of experience, time, and support. As noted above, the value of bringing years of professional training and experience into one room and focusing it on one therapist's case simply cannot be duplicated in any other way. The powerful dynamics of group supervision maximize the resources of a group practice.

Group supervision also helps each participant through the miracle of vicarious learning. Even a staff member who remains quiet during group supervision benefits from the information they hear and the support they witness between other staff members. The problem the group is discussing today, may be the very problem that therapist will encounter tomorrow. Vicarious learning occurs whether a group supervision participant is presenting a case, helping with a case, or learning through their observation of other participants.

Group supervision also allows for multidisciplinary and multitheoretical input. Over time most therapists tend to favor a certain approach to their therapeutic work. Perhaps they feel most comfortable within a medical model, a developmental approach, a family systems perspective, or a psychodynamic understanding of the client's experience. Perhaps a certain viewpoint better matches their personality. Very often, stepping outside of our own biases, assumptions, and blind spots can help us take a fresh look at our own work with a particular client and allow us to be ultimately more help to them.

Group supervision also provides the advantage of tending to several secondary functions of a group practice. It can provide a valuable check and balance mechanism on therapists' clinical work. By presenting a case, asking for feedback, and hearing the input from the other participants, both the presenting member and the other group participants can gage their relative expertise, skill, and ability. This is valuable because it can assist in both the initial case assignment and later in-group referral process. By knowing the relative strengths and limitations of any given member, a better client/therapist match may be made from the start of treatment and more effective in-group referrals can be facilitated.

Finally, group supervision also has the secondary advantage of setting the values and professional tone of the group practice. Groups who adopt the group supervision model do so with a preference for openness and vulnerability, collaborative learning, and continued personal and professional growth. The value of these is not to be understated. They are realized only through the implementation of effective group supervision techniques and a skillful group supervision facilitator.

Discussion Question #2:

What are some of the advantages of group supervision to you?

_____

_____

_____

_____

Limitations

Group supervision may not be the best choice for all group practices. There are several disadvantages to this approach to supervision. The first is time. Since group practices can vary greatly in their number of members, the time allocated for group supervision must be proportionate to the supervision needs of its members. Members' needs are often influenced by the level of their professional development. Younger members may need more time to properly address the range of their concerns, than do more senior members. If too little time is planned, then some group members will become frustrated and the depth of meaningful feedback will be limited. If too much time is devoted to some staff, others may become frustrated. Eventually, members may simply choose not to participate or do so only in a limited or less meaningful fashion.

The limitation of time may not hold true for higher education, however. In fact practicing supervision in triads allows for more diversity of feedback for students and may free up faculty time, otherwise spent in individual supervision. Lonn (2014) provided a review of the triadic supervision literature and noted several other benefits including: vicarious learning, multiple perspectives, improved relationships with peers, and increased sense of trust and safety in the supervision process. Borders, Brown, and Purgason (2015) summarized research that indicated triadic supervision complements individual and group supervision by offering unique opportunities not found in the other supervisory approaches. In professional settings where only a few members wish to participate, smaller group supervision may be expected to retain similar benefits as found in more academically utilized triadic supervision.

Another disadvantage is the need for active participation. Many therapists are by their nature introverted. Others may not feel as confident about sharing their struggles with other group members. Still others may be satisfied sitting on the sidelines and observing. While this does have the benefit of vicarious learning, it may, in time, create an uncomfortable imbalance in group supervision participation. To help guard against this problem, the group may want to rotate case presenters; and the group facilitator may be well advised to solicit everyone's involvement in providing feedback to the presenter. Linton (2003) stated that supervisees in group supervision tend to cushion the feedback instead of being open and honest, thus limiting the potential value of the feedback. If this does occur, the supervisor could make this issue a supervision topic for discussion, encouraging more specific and ultimately helpful feedback.

Of a more ominous nature is the possibility that group supervision may uncover underlying dysfunctional group dynamics. Therapists are, after all, human beings. As such we bring our own stuff to all the groups in which we are members. Sometimes, we, too, can form unconscious alliances, can triangulate other group members, or even sabotage healthy group interaction through our own projections and unhealthy behavior. If group supervision does uncover underlying dysfunctional group dynamics, perhaps it is in the group's long-term best interests to identify it and directly deal with the unhealthy group dynamics.

A final potential disadvantage of group supervision is the risk of the formation of theoretical camps and resulting turf wars. This could monopolize the type and quality of input a presenter might receive or cause the supervision session to descend into a debate on theoretical supremacy. As previously noted, many therapists have their theoretical or specialty-focused preferences. Rather than allow one viewpoint to dominate, it falls upon the group to establish the value of a multidisciplinary and multi-theoretical approach and for the group facilitator to affirm that value by encouraging a variety of feedback. Feedback from multiple theoretical perspectives is often very helpful in expanding awareness and stimulating alternative interventional strategies.

Discussion Question #3:

What other limitations might concern you about group supervision?

_____

_____

_____

_____

Procedures

For years the main method of conducting supervision was individual supervision. In 2001 the Council for Accreditation of Counseling and Related Education Programs (CACREP) approved triadic supervision as an additional method of supervision. Triadic supervision creates a new system with usually one supervisor paired with two supervisees (Hein & Lawson, 2008). Within that system there are numerous methods of conducting supervision. In a study by Nguyen (2004) the differences between a single focus and split focus were examined. Although there were no differences in supervisee's effectiveness between the two types, there was a positive difference in supervisee development with split focus. Single focus supervision has one supervisee sharing a case(s) for one entire session, whereas split focus has both supervisees offering cases equally during the session.

In further research Bakes (2005) investigated the supervisory working alliance in individual and triadic supervision. The results suggested that triadic supervision minimized identification with the supervisor and his/her supervisory perspective but increased the supervisees' understanding of the client and the case. From this work it appears reasonable to assume that increasing the number of participants in supervision from individual, to triadic and group supervision, likely changes the supervisee's focus from the supervisor to the client and the case.

Regardless of the size of the supervision group, several considerations for the supervisor and the supervisee were outlined by Werstlein (1994,

2001). For the supervisor these included: designing the group to involve five to eight supervisees who meet for one to one and half hours on a regular basis; members having some commonalities and diversities with respect to experience or level of professional development; a pre-planned structure to address aspects of focus, content, time and process; an orientation for new group members to discuss expectations and member responsibility; supervisor use of group facilitation skills to manage session content, group process, and member involvement; focus on group peer interaction to promote feedback, support, and encouragement; use of structured case presentation formats; and management of group dynamics to balance potentially competitive tendencies with creativity and spontaneity.

For the supervisee these included: being prepared to listen, get verbally involved, take risks, and share your thoughts and feelings; decrease personalization of frustration with open expression toward group members; intentionally look for similarities in your reactions to group members and your reactions to clients; be ready to move from focus on client dynamics to counselor dynamics; and be specific with what kind of feedback and assistance you are looking for from the group.

When it is time to begin a group supervision session, the first task of the group supervision facilitator is to call the session to order. This may take some doing if you have a busy staff. Once it is established who will be attending the day's session, the door to the room is closed for privacy and the meeting is not interrupted with exception to an emergency situation that would necessarily pull a counselor away. Next the facilitator sets a few ground rules involving issues of confidentiality, the goals of group supervision, the importance of participation, and intent to be respectful and helpful to one another. Then the facilitator surveys the group to determine those who would like to present a case and the general theme of each case to be presented. Sometimes a group member will want to present an entire case. Other times only one particular aspect of a case will be presented for discussion. Next the cases for the day's supervision agenda are prioritized and discussion begins. Prioritizing the day's cases can be challenging. Some considerations include: the needs and developmental level of the supervisee, the immediacy of the presenting issue (suicidal risk, harm toward others, therapeutic impasse, concerns involving outside parties such as employer, spouse, physician, or attorney), the potential value of the case for group learning, and the likely time demands of an unusual or complicated case.

It can be useful when prioritizing the cases to be sure to allow enough time for the depth and complexity of the theme to be discussed. This can be estimated by both the facilitator's experience and the presenting group member's estimate of how much time they will likely need. Brief items are often best addressed first, to clear the slate for the more involved cases. Once the brief items are completed, the remaining time can be allocated to the group members who have requested more in-depth discussion.

Now the group is ready to focus on each individual case. The presenting member is encouraged to share some background information about the case. This can include: demographics, presenting concern, relevant history, family of origin, marital adjustment, risk of abuse, risk of substance abuse, previous treatment, test results, diagnosis, medication, current treatment plan, and response to treatment. Then the facilitator calls for the supervision question. "How can we help you?" "What do you need from us?" "What would you like to get out of supervision today?" The facilitator then encourages group discussion. At the initial stage of discussion, the group members readily offer their feedback. A few are often very verbal and others remain quiet. Once the initial discussion seems to slow, additional comments are solicited from the more quiet members. The facilitator may restate some of the comments, ask more open-ended questions to encourage more discussion, or summarize the general themes of what has been discussed. When the discussion seems to be coming to a close, the facilitator then checks in with the presenting therapist to verify that they received the feedback they were seeking. If an affirmative answer is received, the discussion proceeds to the next case. If not, the facilitator then requests that the presenter restate or refine their question and further discussion is facilitated. Discussion continues until the presenter feels sufficient feedback has been provided, until their allotted time has expired, or until a follow-up plan for additional help is set.

As the supervision session nears its end, the facilitator asks what each supervisee gained from supervision, summarizes the themes of the day, reviews any follow-up tasks, and sets the next supervision session.

All participants are thanked for their participation and the facilitator makes appropriate notes about the supervision session. These notes are useful as they provide a summary of the content of the day, outline any need for follow-up action with the presenting therapist, and provide documentation for any future supervisory, liability, or legal issue that may arise.

Discussion Question #4:

What procedural element, if any, would you add to help the supervision group run more smoothly?

_____

_____

_____

_____

The Facilitator's Role

The primary role of the facilitator is to provide structure for the supervision session. This includes organizing the agenda, managing the time, and maintaining the focus that best seems to meet the presenter's request. The facilitator is also responsible for maintaining an atmosphere that is conducive to open discussion and which encourages group member participation. This is not always easy since some cases will inevitably generate healthy debate, some presenters may express defensiveness, and some feedback may not always be complimentary. It is still vitally important that the facilitator promote an environment that will help group members to speak and case presenters to listen.

New supervision groups, as with other kinds of groups, may initially struggle to achieve a healthy working atmosphere. While the purpose of a supervision group is usually clear, to aid each other in the provision of effective therapy, they may struggle with establishing appropriate norms and fall into periods of unexpected conflict. It is vital in these situations that the supervision group facilitator take the lead in establishing effective group norms and processing any group conflict that may emerge. If this is not done, the task of effective group supervision will not be accomplished.

Discussion Question #5:

In what ways is group supervision like group counseling? Is it appropriate for group members to, at times, assume the facilitator role? Discuss.

_____

_____

_____

_____

Focus of Group Supervision

The focus of group supervision can take many different forms. The most typical is a case presentation intended to seek input on treatment planning and effective interventions. Just as often, however, therapists are looking for help with case conceptualization. They understand the presenting concern, and the client's symptomology, but they struggle to understand the underlying dynamics that maintain the client's undesired behavior. The multidisciplinary and multi-theoretical strengths of group supervision are often very helpful in enhancing case conceptualization.

Group supervision is also a useful forum for providing case updates. Much can be learned from what went well and what went poorly. Some cases can become exemplars and are great examples to illustrate the utility of a certain technique or intervention strategy. Cases that turn out poorly can also be an excellent learning tool. In group supervision, the members can conduct a therapeutic autopsy, reviewing what happened, what did not work, and what might have led to a better outcome.

Group supervision in a community setting has similarities to peer group supervision that recent graduate students have encountered. There are advantages and disadvantages to this type of supervision. A systematic, structured approach seems to alleviate many of the concerns about peer group supervision (Borders, 1991). Granello, Kindsvatter, Granello, Underfer-Babalis and Hartwig Moorhead (2008) write that a supervisory peer consultation group also widens and expands critical thinking and case conceptualization skills in each of the team members. A structured peer group format has the following advantages:

- Ensures all members are involved
- Emphasizes focused and objective feedback

- Emphasizes cognitive counseling skills
- Can be used with groups of experienced and inexperienced counselors
- Provides a framework for supervisors
- Teaches an approach for self-monitoring (Fall & Sutton, 2004).

Structured peer group supervision is the type of supervision that is provided in this chapter's videostreaming demonstration.

Ethical issues can become an important focus of group supervision. Discussions about the risks of dual relationships, involvement of children and family services, duty to warn, confidentiality, client's right to refuse treatment, limits of therapist expertise, and need to refer are only a few of some of the issues with which group supervision can help.

There are also several counselor issues that group supervision can address. These include transference, countertransference, projection, defenses, and other forms of therapeutic bias or distortion that are much more easily seen from outside the therapeutic relationship than within it. Anderson (2008), in writing about psychodynamic group supervision, noted the importance of the supervisee's reactions to client material, the supervisee's reactions to the supervisor and other supervisees, and the enactment of parallel process, where interpersonal dynamics offer an opportunity to understand supervisee's active personal issues and how they may be playing out in both group supervision and their therapeutic relationship with the client. Group supervision can provide a rich, safe, and very helpful environment to identify these dynamics and discuss how they can be harnessed for counselor, client, and group understanding and enrichment.

Sometimes client issues will also affect therapeutic effectiveness. Such considerations as client readiness for change, developmental level of functioning, and sources of client resistance are more readily observable from an outside perspective. In addition, gender, age, and cultural diversity issues can also be explored in supervision. In a Delphi study validating counselor supervision competencies, Neuer Colburn, Grothaus, Hays, and Milliken (2016) highlighted cultural responsiveness as one of five important categories of supervision competence. Within cultural responsiveness were: attention to issues of power and privilege, impact of multicultural influences on the client, respect for diverse values and world views, and discussion of the effects of these influences in supervision and counseling. As therapists we often like to think that we can help everyone who steps through our door but the truth is we are a product of our own gender, age, and cultural background and perhaps the input from a diverse group of colleagues and clients will help us recognize our limits and/ or learn how to more effectively understand and bridge our differences.

In group supervision we can also learn new techniques, new skills, and the latest research findings related to our concern. While our ethics direct us to work within the limits of our own expertise, there are many more subtle techniques and skills that we continuously acquire throughout our years of practice. Group supervision can help us learn and apply these techniques while under the supervision of those who possess them. In addition, group supervision can help keep us informed of the latest research pertaining to our area of focus or specialty. It is very difficult for one individual to keep up with the professional literature but much easier to rely on the collective study of a group of colleagues.

Group supervision can be an invaluable place for learning about the referral sources in your own community. Chances are that more experienced colleagues have great information about the many community resources in your area. Whether these are particular individual practitioners, community programs, or even allied professionals, they know the reputations and can steer you toward the resources that may be most helpful to your clients.

Information about professional development, credentialing, or specialty training is also available from more experienced group supervision members. Who to call, where to pick up an application, necessary requirements, trainers to avoid, and trainers to sign on with, your group supervision members are often a wealthy source of tested professional development information.

Finally, a more mundane but essential aspect of any professional's job is information about administrative issues. What forms are used for what purpose? How do I handle the paperwork? What is our policy about this? How do I handle past due accounts with my clients? These are just some of the administrative questions that can be readily answered through group supervision. Why reinvent the wheel when those who use it on a daily basis are readily available for your consultation?

Discussion Question #6:

What are some issues you would like to address in your group supervision?

_____

_____

_____

_____

Other Important Issues in Group Supervision

Should participation in group supervision be voluntary or mandatory? Most mental health professional associations recommend that its members be actively involved in supervision. They do not necessarily dictate whether that supervision is individual or group. Most group practices attempt to support this recommendation by encouraging their members to participate in ongoing professional supervision, whether individual or group. There are some professionals who take exception to this, feeling that they have enough experience and training and therefore do not need ongoing supervision. This is a shortsighted view of the role of supervision in clinical practice. The value and benefits of supervision are well established. Supervision is a place to get feedback, receive support, become rejuvenated, and most importantly improve one's therapeutic effectiveness. It also provides a rich, professionally diverse context for this to occur.

While in professional practice, supervision has yet to be mandated, under Section C Professional Responsibility, C.2.d. Monitor Effectiveness of the American Counseling Association (ACA, 2014) code of ethics, it states that counselors should continually monitor their effectiveness and take reasonable steps to seek peer supervision to evaluate their efficacy as counselors. Supervision, whether informally sought with peers or more formally engaged in through an organized group format, is one voluntary activity that is essential to guard liability, prevent malpractice, and more positively, to assure continued development of clinical expertise.

Should participation in group supervision be paid or unpaid? Generally speaking, it is always important to value the professional work of another through reasonable remuneration for services rendered. With the collegial atmosphere of group supervision, the roles of case presenter and provider of feedback frequently change within one session. Even the group facilitator who may not be presenting a case benefits from the discussion that unfolds. In many ways all participants of group supervision both contribute to and benefit from it. A common private practice model is that no one is paid for participation in group supervision because no revenue is being generated and all participants receive significant professional benefit. In an agency setting, where staff are paid by salary, group supervision is simply one of the expected job duties and its remuneration is included in staff salaries. Payment for private group supervision, beyond that offered by an agency or a private practice, is typically paid for by the participants and provided by a higher credentialed facilitator. If all participating parties benefit, perhaps payment is not necessary. Payment is a decision that is best determined by review of the various factors in the practice setting.

Documentation is a very important aspect of both individual and group supervision. As in therapy, where paperwork provides a record of the therapeutic process, supervision documentation provides a record of appropriate professional review. In malpractice liability cases, one of the more common professional mistakes is to not have sought supervisory input into a critical treatment issue. Even when one has sought input, it is typically not sufficient to just report that one spoke with their supervisor. Detailed documentation about the nature of the discussion and the resulting action plan or recommendations is the best evidence to validate appropriate professional practice.

One of the more difficult supervisory issues to address is that of an impaired therapist. The process of group supervision sometimes reveals obvious problems with therapist impairment but more often yields subtle indicators that suggest that a therapist may be practicing with a significant personal impairment. Some examples of common therapist impairments include substance abuse, an untreated mental health problem, or significant personal life stressors such as divorce or close family loss that might emotionally overwhelm a therapist and impede their therapeutic objectivity, judgment, and effectiveness. To avoid an undue defensive reaction from the identified impaired therapist, it may be best to provide constructive feedback first in an individual supervision setting.

Once acknowledged and an action plan agreed upon, the matter may be more readily addressed in the group supervision setting. While it is useful to attend to the collegial impact of therapist impairment in the group setting, it is first necessary for the impaired therapist to be able to acknowledge their impairment and take ownership of their personal recovery plan.

Another important issue in group supervision is how the expectations, focus, and form of supervision may change depending upon the employment setting. Typical settings for mental health services include: private practice, school, agency, medical, educational, and business. Each of these settings has a different service population and varies in the type of allied professionals with whom the mental health provider collaborates. The diversity of each of these settings does not allow for a detailed review here but one illustrative example might help the reader appreciate the necessity of attending to these differences. This example involves differences in the assumptions underlying medical versus traditional mental health settings. Most traditional mental health settings view treatment as primarily a one-to-one relationship between a client and a therapist. Most medical health settings view a client's treatment as a team effort. Both settings operate on different assumptions about confidentiality, the comprehensiveness of treatment, and how authority and accountability are handled within the treatment team. Supervision issues are not only about the client/therapist relationship but likely also include the client's physical and perhaps vocational health needs. The individual therapist is not the primary authority for treatment; a nurse, nutritionist, social worker, physician, psychiatrist, etc., together develop and implement the client's treatment plan. Confidentiality in this setting is not reserved only for the individual therapist, it is extended to the treatment team. Sensitivity to the demands of different employment settings and modification of group supervision expectations, focus, and form will make group supervision more effective.

The final important issue in group supervision is its insufficiency in providing the depth of case review that is sometimes necessary to effectively assist a presenting therapist or a group of therapists who want feedback. Group supervision time is often limited; the larger the group, the greater the likelihood that some cases will not be sufficiently reviewed. Some groups deal with this by prioritizing the cases to be presented, asking staff to prepare a summary of their case ahead of time, limiting the time each group member has to present, and by providing ample individual supervision to follow up on any needs that cannot be addressed in the group session. Still other issues sometimes emerge that call for deeper more personal reflection such as those involving transference, counter-transference, projection, or parataxic distortion. In a supervision group with strong trust, emotionally secure therapists, and a skillful facilitator, these issues can be successfully addressed. However, sometimes a therapist may feel inhibited in exploring the personal basis underlying these dynamics in front of their colleagues and would rather and perhaps more effectively do so in individual supervision. Group supervision has many advantages, but its limitations must also be noted.

Discussion Question #7:

Offer your thoughts and feelings about many of the questions asked in this section. In a community and school setting, do you think supervision should be mandatory? Should you get paid as a supervisor? As a counselor?

_____

_____

_____

_____

Group Supervision Video Questions:

Watch the group supervision video and observe the skills discussed in this chapter. There were several supervision questions answered. Particularly observe the interaction of the supervisory team, and the beneficial aspects of having such diverse team members from novice counselors to master-level professionals. Follow the transcripts for additional assistance.

Neurocounseling Implications for Group Supervision

Often group supervision can be fast paced and time limited, so the group facilitator must ensure that the supervisory needs of each member in the group get met. The level of complexity with group supervision is greater as the number of team members increases.

With this added complexity, understanding how the parietal lobes work is important to effective group supervision. During group supervision multimodal interactions are constantly occurring. If healthy regulation occurs in the parietal lobes, the emphasized focus can be on spatial relationships and the many different kinds of interactions happening at once. On the Head Map of Function (Figure 2.1) discussed earlier, take a look at P3, PZ, and P4 toward the top back of the head. PZ works on the concept of praxis or turning theory into action. This part of the brain also assists in the concept of dimensionality or the ability to shift one brain state to another (Chapin & Russell-Chapin, 2014; Siever, 2000, 2018). As the group facilitator illustrates connections between one supervision case to another, the parietal lobes are hard at work. Remember the more exercise certain pathways receive, the stronger they become, positively or negatively, neurons firing together, wire together. Strengthening the parietal lobes will assist in healthier living in all aspects of living.

Chapter Nine Final Discussion Questions:

1. As a supervisor and supervisee, what would be your fears about being a member of group supervision?

_____

_____

_____

_____

2. What is your opinion about lifelong group supervision over your counseling career?

_____

_____

_____

_____

3. How important do you think a skilled group supervision leader is to the effectiveness of the team? What part of the brain do you think is working the hardest in group supervision?

_____

_____

_____

_____

References

American Counseling Association (ACA) (2014). ACA code of ethics and standards of practice. Alexandria, VA: Author.

Anderson, L. (2008). Psychodynamic supervision in a group setting: Benefits and limitations. *Psychotherapy in Australia,* 14(2), 36–41.

Association for Counselor Education and Supervision (ACES). (2011). *Taskforce on best practices in clinical supervision.* Retrieved from www.aceonline.net/wp-content/uploads/2011/10/ACES-Best-Practices-in-clinical-supervision-document-FINAL.pdf. [Google Scholar]

Bakes, A.J. (2005). The triadic working alliance: A comparison of dyadic and triadic supervision models. *Dissertation Abstracts International,* 66(06), 211A.

Borders, L.D. (1991). A systematic approach to peer group supervision. *Journal of Counseling & Development,* 69, 248–252.

Borders, L.D., Brown, J.B., & Purgason, L.L. (2015). Triadic supervision with practicum and internship counseling students: A peer supervision approach. *The Clinical Supervisor,* 34(2), 232–248.

Borders, L.D., Glosoff, H.L., Welfare, L.E., Hayes, D.G., DeKruyf, L., Fernando, D.M., & Page, B. (2014). Best practices in clinical supervision: Evolution of a counseling specialty. *The Clinical Supervisor,* 33(1), 26–44. doi/ref/10.1080/07325223.2014.905225

Chapin, T.J. & Russell-Chapin, L.A. (2014). *Neurotherapy and neurofeedback: Brain-based treatment for psychological and behavioral problems.* New York, NY: Routledge.

Council for Accreditation of Counseling and Related Educational Programs (CACREP). (2015). *CACREP 2016 standards.* Retrieved from www.cacrep.org/wp-content/uploads/2017/08/2016-Standards-with-citations.pdf

Council for Accreditation of Counseling and Related Educational Programs (CACREP). (2001). *Accreditation and procedures manual and application.* Alexandria, VA: Author.

Fall, M. & Sutton, J.M. (2004). *Clinical supervision: A handbook for practitioners.* Boston: Allyn & Bacon.

Granello, D.H., Kindsvatter, A., Granello, P.R., Underfer-Babalis, J., & Hartwig-Moorhead, H. (2008). Multiple perspectives in supervision: Using a peer consultation model to enhance supervisor development. *Counselor Education & Supervision,* 9(48), 32–48.

Hein, S. & Lawson, G. (2008). Triadic supervision and its impact on the role of the supervisor: A qualitative examination of supervisors' perspectives. *Counselor Education & Supervision,* (48), 16–31.

Heller, S.S. & Gilkerson, L. (Eds.). (2009). *A practical guide to reflective supervision.* Washington, DC: Zero to Three.

Hollingsworth, M.A. (2018). *The role of self-regulation and self-care with academic performance.* 8(6), 251–262. Psychology Research. doi:10.17265/2159-5542/2018.06.002.

Kreider, H.D. (2014). Administrative and clinical supervision: The impact of dual roles on supervisee disclosure in counseling supervision. *The Clinical Supervisor*, 33(2), 256–268.

Linton, J.M. (2003). A preliminary qualitative investigation of group processes in group supervision: Perspectives of master's level practicum students. *Journal of Specialists in Group Work*, 28, 215–226.

Lonn, M.R. (2014). *In search of best practices: A review of triadic supervision literature*. Retrieved from www.counselingoutfitters.com/vistas/vistas14article73.pdf

Neuer Colburn, A.A., Grothaus, T., Hays, D.G., & Milliken, T. (2016). A Delphi study and initial validation of counselor supervision competencies. *Counselor Education and Supervision*, 55(1), 2–15. doi.org/10.1002/ceas.12029

Nguyen, T.V. (2004). A comparison of individual supervision and triadic supervision. *Dissertation Abstracts International*, 64(09), 3204A.

Orchowski, L., Evangelista, N.M., & Probst, D.R. (2010). Enhancing supervisee reflectivity in clinical supervision: A case study illustration. *Psychotherapy Theory, Research, Practice, Training*, 47, 51–67.

Ray, D. & Altekruse, M. (2000). Effectiveness of group supervision versus combined group and individual supervision. *Counselor Education and Supervision*, 40(9), 19–30.

Russell-Chapin, L. & Ivey, A. (2004). *Your supervised practicum and internship: Field resources for turning theory into practice*. Pacific Grove, CA: Brooks/Cole.

Siever, D. (2018). Personal communication.

Siever, D. (2000). *The rediscovery of audio-visual entrainment technology*. Comptronic Devices.

Werstlein, P.O. (2001). Group supervision. *Journal of the International Child and Youth Network* (CYC-Net), 28. Retrieved from http://cyc-net.org/cyc-online/cycol-0501-supervision.html

Werstlein, P.O. (1994). *Fostering counselors' development in group supervision*. ERIC Digest, EDO-CG-94-19.

Wolf, C.P., Thompson, I.A., Thompson, E.S., & Smith-Adock, S. (2014). Refresh your mind, rejuvenate your body, renew your spirit: A pilot wellness program for counselor education. *Journal of Individual Psychology*, 70, 57–75. doi: 10.1353/jip.2014.001

10
FUTURE TRENDS IN SUPERVISION

Overview

The field of counseling supervision is in the midst of a golden renaissance due to many professional, economic, social, and technological factors. Counseling licensure has brought a renewed emphasis on maintaining good standards of practice. An emphasis on the role of spirituality and religion as well as professional and client wellness has been encouraged by our accreditation and best practices standards. The high costs of health care, influences of managed care, the Mental Health Parity Act and the Affordable Care Act, with its emphasis on integrating behavioral health with primary care, have brought needed attention to counseling outcomes and efficient management of resources. The growth of counseling specialties and their expansion across many professional settings has generated a need for multidisciplinary approaches and applications. In addition, our society has made several significant cultural shifts. We are growing older and more diverse. Continuing advances in technology have enriched our opportunities for access to remote areas and speedy communication via such modalities as email, cyber-supervision, teleconferencing, and group chat rooms. This final chapter discusses these numerous variables and new directions impacting the field of counseling supervision.

Goals

- Explore new directions in clinical supervision.
- Encourage helping professionals to engage in continued counseling supervision.

Improved Standards of Practice

Counseling licensure is now law in 50 states in America, Puerto Rico, and the District of Columbia (ACA, 2019). With it has come minimum educational standards and regulated supervision experience. Borders et al. (2014) defined a set of best practices in clinical supervision and suggested useful strategies for their implementation. Many states have begun to mandate continuing education to focus primarily on the critical issues surrounding counseling supervision. While continuing education is a good thing, many of these efforts have fallen short. They often require a set amount of classroom hours about supervision but frequently do not require continuation of direct counseling supervision after professional licensure.

It is the authors' opinion that required continuation of direct counseling supervision, post-licensure, is on the horizon. When it arrives, recommended continuing supervision will give way to mandated post-licensure supervision. This will strengthen the profession and improve standards of practice.

Discussion Question #1:

Do you believe that mandatory supervision should be required of all licensed professionals? Explain.

_____

_____

_____

_____

Spirituality

In a survey from The Polling Report (2004), 92 percent of the responders acknowledge that they believe in God. Other national surveys reveal a high proportion of the population believes in something outside of themselves, a transcendent force (Aten & Hernandez, 2004). It makes sense, then, that counselors and supervisors will have clients with religious and spiritual concerns (Berkel, Constantine, & Olson, 2007). It also makes sense that supervisees and supervisors will have personal religious and spiritual concerns. Unfortunately few graduate level programs offer systematic training on religious/spiritual matters (Russell & Yarhouse, 2006; Conway, 2005; Brawer, Handal, Fabricatore, Roberts, & Wajda-Johnston, 2002; Young, Cashwell, Wiggins-Frame, & Belair, 2002) and very little information occurs in the supervision literature on this matter (Bishop, Avila-Juarbe, & Thumme, 2003). However, according to Hicks (2009), helping supervisees in understanding their own personal beliefs, morals, and prejudices about different faiths is the first step in working effectively with those of different faiths. Much like other areas of diversity, exploring the client's and/or supervisee's personal view and experience at the outset is an essential way to build understanding and respect with those of diverse faiths.

While the importance of spirituality is often included as part of a counselor education wellness training program, unfortunately, it appears there is much more to be done toward more effectively integrating spirituality and religion into counselor education programs. Adams, Puig, Baggs, and Pence Wolf (2015) suggested that despite the general recognition for the need, significant barriers remain. These include lack of information, interest, or perceived relevance within the counselor education curriculum. Future trends in counselor supervision are likely to focus on this often missing factor.

Discussion Question #2:

Why does religion and spirituality seem to cause us such distress even in the realm of supervision?

_____

_____

_____

_____

Wellness

As previously noted in this book, the Council for Accreditation of Counseling and Related Educational Programs (CACREP, 2015) has highlighted the importance of wellness training for professional counselors and now requires counselor education programs to provide wellness education to counseling trainees in order to both prevent professional burnout and to encourage wellness in their clients (Meany-Walen, Davis-Gage, & Lindo, 2016). One session of wellness training is not sufficient. The "Best Practices in Clinical Supervision" recommend that supervisors routinely assess supervisees' level of wellness and their ability to provide effective care to their clients (Association for Counselor Education and Supervision, 2011). Many wellness models exist in the literature but most describe one's intentional movement toward optimal health and integration of physical, intellectual, emotional, life work, social, and spiritual dimensions. Chapin (2017) wrote about neurological factors involved in creating wellness and optimal performance. These included attention to focus time, playtime and downtime, physical time and sleep time, social connecting time, time in emotion expression and spiritual practice, lifestyle changes in nutrition, weight management, sufficient sleep, limited screen time, exercise, and the use of biofeedback for emotional regulation and neurofeedback for optimal neurological regulation.

A very important future trend in clinical supervision will be increased focus on supervisee wellness and optimal performance. With increased demand for counseling services and increased expectations to tend to the wellness of our clients, knowledge, skill, and daily practice in wellness activities is essential.

Discussion Question #3:

What can you do to improve your personal wellness?

_____

_____

_____

_____

Live Supervision

Most counseling supervision is done well after the counselor and client have ended their sessions. This postmortem approach does allow the counselor and supervisor to review session recordings, reflect on what has transpired, and strategize new approaches for the next session. This approach, however, does not allow for timely feedback to the counselor which could be used as immediate input on the counseling session.

Champe and Kleist (2003) reviewed 12 years of research on live clinical supervision and concluded that it appears to be a stable and largely understood method of clinical supervision with some concern about its use with respect to the developmental level of the trainee and some debate about the optimal number of calls during a session and the number of suggestions offered by the supervisor. Rousmaniere and Fredrickson (2016) further refined the use of live clinical supervision, by adapting its use with the latest computer technology. They described their process as remote live supervision, a videoconference for one-way mirror supervision. They suggested that this method greatly expanded the accessibility of clinical training by providing live supervision for a supervisee anywhere in the world. They added that it appears beneficial for both early trainees and those in advanced clinical training.

In addition to the value of immediate feedback for therapeutic interventions, live supervision can also be utilized by doctoral and master's level students working conjointly with faculty in "supervision of supervision." That is learning how to conduct clinical supervision. In one unique arrangement, pre-doctoral psychology interns working with master level social work interns were paired. This allowed for greater flexibility, disruption of stubborn assumptions, and further personal growth opportunities (Haber, Marshall, Cowan, Vanlandingham, Gerson, & Fitch, 2009).

Live, immediate feedback supervision appears to offer many advantages over delayed, after-the-session supervisory feedback. While some limitations in office construction and access to technology may inhibit its use, live supervision appears to be a future trend in counseling supervision, especially for counseling trainees.

Discussion Question #4:

How do you think you would respond in a live supervision situation?

_____

_____

_____

Adaptation of Training Models with Advances in Technology

Numerous models of supervision are presented in the previous chapters. One early model, based in family therapy supervision, relied on old but effective real-time technology. Originally developed by Steve DeShazer (1985), Brief Strategic Therapy was taught through *in vivo* (live) case supervision. Their training room was simply equipped with a one-way mirror and a direct line telephone to the therapy room. Typically one or more supervisors with other students in training observed live therapy from behind a one-way mirror. At certain key moments, a call may come in from the observation room with suggested counseling interventions, which the counselor may immediately deliver to the client. In addition, once the session was completed, it could be immediately debriefed. This supervisory style has been further modified by other more advanced technologies.

Receiving immediate feedback through technology has many advantages over the traditional delayed, supervision model. First, the critical moment is not lost. Second, many eyes, ears, and minds can be focused on the therapy material, allowing for greater depth and creativity to be harnessed for the client's benefit. Third, feedback to the counselor is immediate and its impact instantly observable. However, many counseling offices and training centers are not designed to allow for one-way mirror observation and direct communication from supervisee to supervisor.

The future will likely see expansion of this approach because its impact is so profound. Distance learning is a large part of higher education and is an integral aspect of many health care curricula and clinics (Adams, Tarolli, & Dorsey, 2017). Layne and Hohenshil (2005) assert that technology in counseling and supervision is here to stay and counseling training programs must provide the necessary workshops and courses to assist supervisees and supervisors in its effective use (Vaccaro & Lambie, 2007).

Other technological advancements involve interactive simulations to assist supervisees and supervisors in building skills (Baltimore, Fitch, & Gillam, 2005; Dufrene & Tanner, 2008, Manzanares, O'Halloran, McCartney, Filer, Varhely, & Calhoun, 2004). Today's cell phone technology has allowed for the use of counseling apps to provide basic intervention for those struggling with anxiety, depression, eating, and sleep problems (Bakker, Kazantzis, Rickwood, & Rickwood, 2016). Studies indicate that email, computer-based teleconferencing, electronic mailing lists, chat rooms, computer-assisted live supervision, videoconferencing, and other cyber-supervision strategies are being implemented in many counseling and social work training programs (Harvey & Carlson, 2003; Panos, 2005). To assess the effectiveness of these strategies, Damianakis, Climans and Maziali (2008) used data from a four-year study of web-based video conferencing with caregiver groups and weekly supervision. Even though users experienced some technological difficulties, results of the cyber-supervision group were consistent with those in face-to-face group settings.

Advances in technology have touched the counseling profession and have profound implications for facilitating new and exciting opportunities for counseling supervision. Not only can individuals communicate immediately online with email and the Internet, but groups can also interact in real time to allow for true synchronous learning. Distance, time, and cost are all better managed to serve the needs of the client, supervisee, and supervisors (Watson, 2003, 2005; Mallen, Vogel, & Rochlen, 2005). However, as technology advances, we must be aware of the "technologically caused generation gap between new and established workers" (Csiernik, Furze, Dromgole, & Rishchynski, (2006, p. 9). There will need to be a concerted effort to bridge that gap to help the so-called "digital immigrants" catch up with the "digital natives."

Other technological advances include direct video streaming that allows the user to download files, permitting clients in distant settings to access mental health services via online video conferencing. Of course, computer technology is not without its problems. The equipment is expensive, communication between sites requires coordination and is sometimes disrupted, and some people remain reluctant to trust the technology or lack the technical skills to efficiently use it. The issues of confidentiality and privacy become even more complicated when using technology. The use of encrypted or secure transmission of supervisory information is essential (Shaw & Shaw, 2006) and the need to guard the environmental privacy of the user is ever present.

The future of counseling supervision will no doubt capitalize on the benefits of these technologies for both individual and group supervision. They are efficient and useful tools for written, spoken, and visual communications (Kennedy, 2008).

Discussion Question #5:

Are you a digital immigrant or digital native? Share your beliefs about the advances in technology and its efficacy in counseling and supervision.

Multidisciplinary Supervision

No longer do counselors work only in small groups with other therapists. They work in schools with teachers and administrators, health care settings with physicians and nurses, in churches with ministers and lay church employees, and in agencies comprised of multidisciplinary professionals. It is not uncommon for an agency or group practice to include counselors, social workers, psychologists, psychiatrists, other medical personnel, and paraprofessional volunteers. Current emphasis on the integration of counseling with primary care in support of client mental health needs and their ability to comply with ongoing medical treatment for such conditions as diabetes and heart disease will continue to drive multidisciplinary supervision (Reisinger Walker, McGee, & Druss, 2015).

This diversity of perspectives is deeply enriching, but it creates increased opportunity for philosophical differences, turf battles, and professional arrogance to impede the supervisory process. Davys and Beddoe (2008) conducted a small qualitative investigation on interprofessional supervision and discovered that rather than hindering the learning process, the diversity of disciplines seemed, "to enhance the breadth of learning and participants were challenged to clarify ideas and language" (p. 68).

Despite our differences, the future will likely bring an influx of multidisciplinary supervision, and this will be a positive development in the helping fields. While great skill will be needed to successfully facilitate multidisciplinary supervision, the benefits far outweigh the potential disadvantages. Multidisciplinary supervision can build cohesiveness. It can allow an individual therapist the opportunity for alternative perspectives. It can also reduce the costs associated with more traditional one-on-one, face-to-face supervision.

Discussion Question #6:

What are the supervisory benefits in having a multidisciplinary approach?

_____

_____

_____

_____

Group Supervision

As the barriers of post-licensure counseling supervision diminish, more and more professionals will seek ongoing counseling supervision. While many will likely continue to prefer a one-on-one supervision relationship, more will seek group supervision opportunities. Group supervision has many advantages over individual supervision (Ray & Altekruse, 2000). It pools the experiences and resources of several professionals and allows all to learn from vicarious and direct participation in the supervision process.

Borders et al. (2014) noted that group supervision should not be chosen solely because it is convenient for the supervisor. It is chosen if it is determined to maximize involvement and constructive feedback and is not detrimental to the supervisees involved. In today's high pressure workplace, with increasing client caseloads and limited time for supportive assistance, group supervision is likely to be seen as a value-rich alternative.

Group supervision may not be for everyone. It requires a certain level of personal confidence, security, and vulnerability to be effective. To "bare your soul" in front of your colleagues is no small task, but the benefits are great. For further information on group supervision, go back to Chapter Nine on group supervision.

Group supervision can provide an expanded professional support network. It can save both time and cost, as many professionals can benefit from the same supervision session, share their rich experience and expertise, and reduce the costs associated with more traditional individual supervision. In today's world of ever-increasing direct service hours and increasing standards of practice, group supervision is sure to have an increased appeal to many professionals.

The social work profession has a wonderful history of conducting their work in small groups. The idea of "partnered practice" in which the transfer of knowledge among and between groups in therapy and supervision may well become an essential part of future clinical supervision (Aronoff & Bailey, 2005) for all of us.

Discussion Question #7:

What are your concerns about participating in group supervision?

_____

_____

_____

_____

Multicultural Focus and Advocacy

As the texture of our society changes, so too, does the skill base needed to successfully counsel the increasingly diverse clients who seek our services. Today's clients are as diverse as the tapestry of America and the world. They are multicultural: African American, Asian, Caucasian, Latino/a, Hispanic, Indian, and Middle Eastern. They are sexually diverse: heterosexual, bi-sexual, transsexual, and homosexual. They are rich and poor, educated and uneducated, male and female, and young and old. They are with privilege or history of oppression, ability status, country of origin, personal history of immigration or native experience, political perspective, world view, spirituality, religion and values.

Counseling supervision must be aware of these diverse needs, communication styles, differing beliefs and values. Our basic counseling theories and practices are not enough. A recent social constructionist model of supervision suggests that there needs to be two distinct goals in assisting supervisees and supervisors in becoming culturally relevant. The first goal is to better understand our differences rather than striving to be culturally competent. The second is to encourage "insiders" (Hair & O'Donoghue, 2009, p. 70) to create their own directives in supervision.

Multicultural sensitivity and awareness are not enough. Borders et al. (2014) presented several considerations in the best practices of diversity and advocacy including attention to clients with minority status, social justice issues, and barriers to services. In today's increasingly polarized society with politically distinct "conservative" and "liberal" camps, wide-ranging displays of racially focused bias, increasing anti-immigration sentiment, and exposure of sexually exploitive and oppressive behavior, the role of advocacy in counseling and counselor supervision has never been greater.

Our future requires that we become citizens of the world, expand our knowledge of diverse populations, and engage opportunities to advocate for those with less influence and power. In addition, we need to appreciate the ever-expanding role that advocacy and social justice may play in the many environments in which we work. We can provide a positive influence both within and outside the counseling relationship by helping to shape the policies, promote access, and improve the treatment of diverse populations in the communities, schools, and workplaces in which we reside. Counseling supervision can play a significant role in helping to address these issues by encouraging healthy human development across an ever-increasing expanse of social settings.

Discussion Question #8:

In what ways could you advocate for a diverse population?

_____

_____

_____

_____

Geriatric Populations

We are getting older. By the year 2020, it is estimated that there will be 56.1 million people who are considered elderly. The census data indicates that individuals 65 and older are the fastest growing segment of the American population (Vespa, Armstrong, & Medina, 2018). Therefore there will continue to be an increased demand for all helping professionals including counselors, social workers, psychologists, and other health care professionals (Rizzo & Rowe, 2006). For social workers alone, the demand is expected to increase 12 percent from 2014 to 2024, faster than the average for all occupations, and the need for mental health and substance abuse counselors to increase 19 percent over the same time frame (U.S. Department of Labor, Bureau of Labor Statistics, 2014). Not only are we older, but we are generally more literate than any previous generation. This has drastic implications for the counseling profession. The needs of the geriatric population have been well documented. They include: transitions from work to retirement, more activity to less, ample to fixed incomes, family focus to marital refocus, eventual change and loss, health and decline, and everyday life "adjustments" (Kampfe, 2015). Everything changes as we age, and the nature of our youth-focused culture is not easily sustained as we age. This is the challenge we all face.

Certification programs are springing up to specifically address the issues faced by this aging population. Counseling supervisors and their supervisees would be well advised to seek out those programs and arm themselves with the tools they need to help address these trends. The research overwhelmingly indicates that healthy aging is the rule not the exception. It is imperative that as helping professionals we prepare ourselves to meet the needs of this aging population.

Discussion Question #9:

Are the helping professions doing enough to prepare current and new counselors to deal with the aging population? How might this impact supervision?

_____

_____

_____

_____

Evidence-Based Treatment

Almost 30 years ago when managed care extended its reach to mental health services, one of its primary goals was to assess and improve the outcomes of mental health treatment. Outcomes were measured by both reduced costs and successfully achieved therapy goals. At the time this sent shock waves through a profession that cherished the privacy of the counseling relationship and subjective nature of therapeutic outcomes.

Today, in many respects, things have come full circle. We have learned from our managed care colleagues how to pay closer attention to therapeutic outcomes and counseling outcome research (Elliott, 2002). We establish specific treatment goals, we provide a DSM-5 (American Psychiatric Association, 2013) or ICD-10-CM (World Health Organization, 2018) diagnosis, and many of us use standardized measures of both the therapeutic relationship and therapeutic outcomes through simple pre-/post-therapy paper and pencil checklists or more sophisticated computerized software programs.

Although many managed care companies have let up on their more rigid functions such as external treatment plan documentation, reauthorization providers, and limited treatment authorizations, the counseling profession continued to focus on "evidence-based treatment" (APA Presidential Task Force on Evidence-Based Practice, 2006) or "What works for whom and when?" Building on the work of Lambert and Barley (2001) that emphasized the quality of the therapeutic relationship, other researchers found little difference in the form of therapy used and instead turned their attention to fitting the form of therapy to the client's particular needs (Norcross, 2011). A future trend in counseling supervision will be continued refinement of therapeutic techniques and procedures and their applications for specific clients with specific problems. The need to know that what we are doing is effective, with whom, will go far in improving our standards of care.

Stoltenberg and Pace (2007, 2008) discussed the need for competency-based supervision approaches that can be viewed as extensions of the counseling skills models that flourished in the late 1960s and 1970s. The need for defining what competency-based skills look like and what defines competency-based supervision is clearly where the supervision field is headed (Falendar & Shafranske, 2007, 2004).

The Microcounseling Supervision Model (MSM) illustrated in Chapter Seven of this book is an excellent example of competency-based supervision (Russell-Chapin, 2007). Another essential dimension of competency-based supervision is to ask supervisees, "to investigate and use approaches and interventions that have some empirically established rationale or lacking that, strong theoretical grounding, and then assess how and why this approach works or doesn't work for them when implemented with a given client" (Stoltenberg & Pace, 2007).

Another focus in the area of evidence-based practice in supervision involves the use of client feedback in supervision (Reese et al., 2009). With ongoing feedback from the client on the counseling relationship and problem improvement, actual client feedback can provide the supervisee a valuable check on the efficacy of their work. This can more immediately enable interventional changes that can benefit the client and maximize the supervisee's learning experience.

Discussion Question #10:

How does evidence-based treatment inform competency-based supervision?

_____

_____

_____

_____

Brain-Based Interventions

In the last decade there have been many advances in brain research and understanding how and why the brain functions. This research debunks some old ideas, validates other existing beliefs, and offers new and encouraging interventions for helping people grow and learn. All of this information has many new implications for the field of counseling and counseling supervision.

For years educators and helping professionals believed that the brain matured around 12 years of age. Now with the help of functional magnetic resonance imaging (fMRI), researchers know that the adolescent brain is fully developed by around 25 years of age or older. However neuroscientists now understand that the brain has the capability to adapt and develop new living neurons up until the very end of our lives according to Dr. Norman Doidge (2007), a psychiatrist at Columbia University Center for Psychoanalytic Training and Research in New York. This process is called neuroplasticity. "Neuroplasticity can result in the wholesale remodeling of neural networks … a brain can rewire itself," states author Norman Doidge, in his book *The Brain that Changes Itself*, p. 16.

The brain is no longer considered a stagnant organ but three-pounds of plastic, fluid, and malleable tissue. Human beings can change their brains and develop new pathways through repetition and learning new skills. Challenging the brain with new tasks such as learning a foreign language can forge different pathways in the brain. The capacity to restructure the brain allows our "brain span" to match our "life span." The old adage, "You can't teach an old dog new tricks," no longer holds true. This information is so important to the field of counseling and supervision because it explains through empirical evidence why counseling works. Through MRI research we can visually see pre- and post-test evidence that shows the impact of counseling on the brain. With negative plasticity the neuronal pathways often lead to faulty thoughts and behaviors. Through new thoughts and practice patterns, clients' brains are encouraged, over time, to construct new neuronal pathways (positive plasticity) and change the brain toward healthier functioning (Schwartz & Begley, 2003). This applies to clients, counselors, supervisees, and supervisors. We are all capable of great change throughout our lives.

New insights from neuroscience have also helped us understand that emotional dysregulation is as much a physiological as a psychological process (Porges, 2011), and healthy self-regulation is made more possible by harnessing the healing potential of physiological and behavioral interventions. Some of these include biofeedback for peripheral skin temperature and heart rate variability training and neurofeedback for retraining the brain's electrical activity associated with a variety of emotional, cognitive, and behavioral problems (Chapin & Russell-Chapin, 2014). Field, Jones, and Russell-Chapin (2017) in their work on neurocounseling directly applied the science of neurophysiology to a wide range of counseling-related topics including: social and cultural implications, trauma, the counseling relationship, theory, assessment, wellness and optimal performance, substance abuse, group work, career counseling, and research. They proposed that knowledge of brain-based interventions, "will forever change how you approach case conceptualization, assessment, and intervention in clinical practice" (p. xiii).

Supervision in neurocounseling and neurofeedback focuses on the effective utilization of specialized knowledge, equipment, and computer technology and its integration within a traditional counseling treatment plan. As you know, the authors of this book thought it was so important to discuss neurocounseling that a section on Neurocounseling and Its Implications for Supervision has been included in each of the preceding chapters.

This specialized knowledge can be gained through coursework and/or certification training programs in biofeedback and neurofeedback approved by the Biofeedback Certification International Alliance (BCIA: www.BCIA.org/). BCIA certification training requires completion of a separate 36-hour didactic and experiential training for biofeedback and 46-hour program for neurofeedback. Board certification in each specialty is also available and involves completion of casework, mentoring, a course in neuroanatomy, and written examination. Learning how to apply biofeedback and neurofeedback within a traditional counseling treatment plan requires knowledge and experience in neurocounseling techniques and strategies (Chapin & Russell-Chapin, 2014; Field et al., 2017). Once learned, effective strategies and considerations for implementing these modalities in an existing counseling practice can be applied (Chapin, 2016).

Future counseling supervision will include increased attention to the physiological and neurological influences on behavior. These, combined with more traditional therapeutic interventions, will likely increase counseling efficacy, decrease client reliance on medication, and strengthen client ability for healthy self-regulation.

With the expanding knowledge and application of brain research to our understanding of human behavior and its implications for counseling intervention come numerous new questions. How will this information be best utilized within the counseling relationship? How will our definition of therapeutic efficiency change? How can we become proficient in combining both traditional and neurologically based interventions? Counseling supervision will provide a valuable venue for exploring these and other yet unformed questions in the use of brain-based intervention in counseling.

Discussion Question #11:

What long-standing beliefs about counseling and supervision will be challenged by advances in brain research?

_____

_____

_____

_____

Increasing Demand

Another future trend is the ever-increasing demand for counseling services, the pressure to hold insurance reimbursement rates low, work with Medicare and Medicaid, and the increasingly difficult time counselors have in maintaining their previous levels of income (Rizzo & Rowe, 2006). As a profession, we have entered a time of both unprecedented opportunity and risk, due to our demonstrated success and value in helping reduce mental illness, and the promise that the provision of relatively inexpensive mental health services can help reduce the continued escalation of U.S. health care costs.

With the passing of both the Mental Health Parity and Addiction Equity Act of 2008 that required the same deductibles, copayments, and limits on visits for mental health as offered for medical health plans, and the passing of the Affordable Care Act of 2010 that required mental health and substance abuse services as one of ten essential benefits, counselors and other mental health providers have come into great demand. The U.S. Health Resources & Services Administration (2016) has estimated that the nation will need 10,000 new providers by 2025. Given current trends, it is likely that these providers will work in close alignment with primary health care providers in hospital-based settings. While this likely assures a steady flow of clients for counselors to see, the risk for counselors is that they may become overworked with high client load demands and may be paid a comparatively lower salary than current traditional private practice models.

While mental health services account for only less than 1 percent of the total U.S. health care budget, the insurance reimbursement rates for mental health services have been steadily declining over the last ten years. This creates a difficult dilemma for mental health providers. If they work for a hospital in a primary care setting, they can expect a high case load and lower pay. If they work in private practice they can expect a decreasing referral base, with still relatively higher but steadily declining insurance reimbursement rates.

As previously noted, the counseling profession has done a great job in demonstrating its effectiveness and value but the increased demand for services and the continuing financial drain on the U.S. health care system will likely "put the squeeze" on the counseling profession. Something has to give, and the trend suggests it will be the counseling professional.

Many counselors chose their profession as a vocational calling. They wanted to help others. Increased demand and reduced insurance reimbursement have already forced many to find other sources of income. Some augment their clinical caseload with fee for service consultation work. Some seek administrative positions. Some teach. Others are closing their practices altogether. New professionals will likely be attracted to the security of a hospital-based, primary care supported, practice that offers a steady but relatively lower income. Increased demand for counseling services presents a potential crisis for professional counselors. Counseling supervision will likely play an important role in helping counselors manage the risk of burnout, facilitating their effective interaction with medical health care providers and in supporting their professional development as they mature and navigate their changing career needs. Supervision throughout the life span of our counseling careers could support us through this challenging time (Russell-Chapin, 2007).

Discussion question #12:

How do you think the increasing demand for counseling will affect counseling supervision?

_____

_____

_____

_____

Professionalization of Supervision

The final future direction in counseling supervision is the continuing professionalization through professional organizations, the establishment of standards of practice, specialized training programs, and required continuing education in supervision for licensed professionals. Borders et al. (2014) detailed current best practices in clinical supervision. These included detailed guidelines for initiating supervision, goal-setting, giving feedback, conducting supervision, the supervisory relationship, diversity and advocacy considerations, ethical considerations, documentation, evaluation, supervision format, the supervisor and supervisor preparation. While supervision beyond education and licensure is still not mandated, the future may hold stronger recommendations about the value of continued supervision throughout one's professional career.

In addition, also strongly recommended will be the use of written supervision policies, supervision plans, and professional wills. These documents clarify all expectations of supervision for the supervisee and supervisor, offer directions for supervision, and ensure that clients' and colleagues' needs are met if some unexpected tragedy happens to the helping professional. An example of a supervision policy and supervision plan outline are provided in Chapter One and an example of a professional will is shown below. These are the documents the authors use in their private practice. It has been the authors' experience that practitioners, clients, other members of a group practice and their family members deeply appreciate the value of clinical supervision and the direction offered by a professional will in the case of a sudden death or disability (Ragusea, 2002). A Clinical Supervision Policy spells out specifically what is expected in supervision from the supervisor, supervisee, and other team members. The Supervision Plan offers unique direction for the specific needs of the supervisee. The Professional Will is a provision that gives authority and explicit instructions to a professional executor. It documents essential information regarding the private practice or agency and the responsible management of clients and their records. The executor of a professional will is usually a mental health colleague who knows the counselor and agency well. Holloway (2003) outlines a few additional topics for inclusion: current and past client records, billing and financial information, appointment book location, email addresses and needed passwords, keys, location of files, patient notification, liability insurance policy numbers, and how to notify the carrier of the malpractice insurance.

Professional Will or Executor Instructions

for the Disposition of Clients of _____, in the
Event of Death, Disappearance or Disability

A. The Professional Executor:

_____ and/or

The Staff of XYZ Inc.
Location:
Phone:

B. My Attorney:

_____
_____
_____
_____

C. My Accountant:

_____
_____
_____
_____

D. General Information:

- Office Location: _____
- Keys to my office and file cabinets are located: _____
  _____
- Closed client files are located: _____
- Open client files are kept: _____
- My personal appointment book is kept: _____
  _____
- Billing Records are kept by the Professional Executor.
- License, malpractice policy and managed care contracts are kept by the Professional Executor.

- All client records must be handled only by the Professional Executor.
- The Professional Executor will assist in notification and/or therapeutic issues to be addressed with my clients.
- Billing issues, insurance and other administrative details already handled by the Professional Executor will continue to be handled by them.

E. Specific Instructions to the Professional Executor

1. In the event I am unable to work for more than two weeks but can communicate effectively, please contact me about how to proceed. Whatever we discuss at that time will take precedence over this document.

2. In the event of my death, disappearance or in the event of temporary or permanent decisional incapacitation, the Professional Executor should take the following steps:

   a. Telephone all scheduled clients and notify them of my current circumstances. Assess clients' need for ongoing therapy. After review of my treatment notes and your telephone assessment, make professional referrals as appropriate. If the client accepts the referral, please obtain the client's consent to release the records to the designated therapist. Please attend to insurance or managed care needs requirements.

   b. When clinically appropriate, please offer my clients one face-to-face contact to process my death or incapacitation with them. If they cannot afford it or the insurance company denies such a session, cover the costs from my outstanding earned salary or bill my estate.

3. Copies of referred clients' records should be forwarded to their new therapists. All remaining records should be maintained and/or destroyed as is customary by the Professional Executor and as advised by the guidelines of the American Psychological Association.

4. Please defer to my designee _____ or executor of my estate _____, any financial decisions to be made regarding outstanding bills or compensation that is due. If a review of the clinical file is needed to ascertain the outstanding

earnings due, please conduct such a review and inform my estate executor of the resulting amounts.

5. Please notify in writing all managed care or insurance companies of my circumstances.

6. There are three copies of this Professional Executor Instructions. The first is located with my other personal papers _____. The second is held by the Professional Executor. The third is on file with my attorney.

7. Charge my estate for the cost of professional time and other reasonable expenses incurred as the result of these instructions.

8. This professional living will is established and shall be governed by the laws of the state of Illinois. I intend that this power of attorney be universally recognized and admissible in any jurisdiction.

_____   _____
Therapist   Date

_____   _____
Professional Executor   Date

_____   _____
Witness   Date

Discussion Questions #13:

1. How will supervision policies involving a Professional Will and Supervision Plan assist in professionalizing the field of supervision?

_____

_____

_____

_____

_____

2. In your opinion, are these policies even necessary?

_____

_____

_____

_____

Summary

Professional, economic, social, and technological factors have impacted the development of counseling supervision. Most of the future trends speak to a promising new era, however a few challenges remain. The momentum is building to ride the wave of reduced stigma, unprecedented access, and the continued professionalization of supervision. The challenges are real. How do we establish a code of conduct among all mental health workers that value the role of continuing post-licensure supervision? How do we navigate the economic pressures that have increased our workload and decreased our salaries? How do we maintain our professional health and wellness? How do we effectively equip ourselves with the knowledge and skills to service a diverse and changing population? And how do we take advantage of the incredible opportunities of technological advances while remaining a human, relationship-oriented profession? The answers to these questions will shape our future and the future of counseling supervision.

The Association for Counselor Education and Supervision of the American Counseling Association, Division 16 of the American Psychological Association and the National Association of Social Workers are all working diligently to elevate and promote the status and role of the clinical supervisor in their respective professional associations. The future of counseling supervision is bright. It is likely that the next five to ten years will see a substantial increase in the number of full-time professional counseling supervisors. We are witnessing the maturation of counseling supervision as a profession. The challenge is up to each of us to seek and accept the best type of supervision (Baird, 2002) and to implement the best practices defined by our profession (Borders et al., 2014).

Chapter Ten Final Questions:

1. What other factors may influence the provision of effective counselor supervision?

_____

_____

_____

_____

2. Which of the discussed trends fit with your supervision needs?

_____

_____

_____

_____

References

Adams, C.M., Puig, A., Baggs, A., & Pence Wolf, C. (2015). Integrating religion and spirituality into counselor education: Barriers and strategies. *Counselor Education and Supervision, 54*(1), 44–56. doi:org/10.1002/j.1556–6978.2015.00069.x

Adams, J.L., Tarolli, C.G., & Dorsey, E.R. (2017). Next generation house call. In Bill Glover (Ed.), *Cerebrum: Emerging ideas in brain science* (pp. 15–24). New York, NY: Dana Press.

American Counseling Association (2019). Licensure. Retrieved January 2019 from www.counseling.org

American Psychiatric Association (2013). *Diagnostic and Statistical Manual-5.* Arlington, VA: American Psychiatric Publishing.

American Psychological Association (APA), Presidential Task Force on Evidence-Based Practice (2006). Evidence-based practice in psychology. *American Psychologist, 61*(4), 271–285. doi:10.1037/0003–066x61.4.271

Aronoff, N. & Bailey, D. (2005). Partnered practice: Building on our small group tradition. *Social Work with Groups, 28*(1), 23–39.

Association for Counselor Education and Supervision (ACES). (2011). *Taskforce on best practices in clinical supervision.* Retrieved from www.aceonline.net/wp-content/uploads/2011/10/ACES-Best-Practices-in-clinical-supervision-document-FINAL.pdf. [Google Scholar]

Aten, J.D. & Hernandez, B.C. (2004). Addressing religion in clinical supervision: A model. *Psychotherapy: Theory, Research, Practice, Training, 41*(2), 152–160.

Baird, B.N. (2002). *The internship, practicum, and field placement handbook* (3rd ed.). Upper Saddle River, NJ: Prentice Hall.

Bakker, D., Kazantzis, N., Rickwood, D., & Rickwood, N. (2016). Mental health smartphone apps: Review and evidence-based recommendations for future developments. *JMIR Mental Health, 3*(1). doi:10.2196/mental.4984

Baltimore, M.L., Fitch, T., & Gillam, L. (2005). Interactive CD-ROM development for use in research: A study of clinical supervision. *Journal of Technology in Counseling, 4*(1). Retrieved January 2009, http://jtc.colstate.edu/Vol4_1/Index.htm

Berkel, L.A., Constantine, M.D., & Olson, E. (2007). Supervisor multicultural competence: Addressing religious and spiritual issues with counseling students in supervision. *The Clinical Supervisor, 26*(1/2), 3–15.

Bishop, D.R., Avila-Juarbe, E., & Thumme, B. (2003). Recognizing spirituality as an important faction in counselor supervision. *Counseling and Values, 48*(10), 34–46.

Borders, D.L., Glosoff, H.L., Welfare, L.E., Hays, D.G., DeKruyf, L., Fernando, D.M., & Page, B. (2014). Best practices in clinical supervision: Evolution of a counseling specialty. *The Clinical Supervisor, 33*(1), 26–44.

Brawer, P.A., Handal, P.J., Fabricatore, A.N., Roberts, R., & Wajda-Johnston, V.A. (2002). Training and education in religion/spirituality within APA-accredited clinical psychology programs. *Professional Psychology: Research and Practice, 33*(2), 203–206.

Champe, J. & Kleist, D.M. (2003). Live supervision: A review of the research. *The Family Journal, 11*(3), 268–275. doi:10.1177/1066480703252755

Chapin, T.J. (2017). Wellness and optimal performance. In T.A. Field, L.K. Jones, & L.A. Russell-Chapin (Eds.), *Neurocounseling: Brain-based clinical approaches* (pp. 133–146). Alexandria, VA: American Counseling Association.

Chapin, T.J. (2016). Developing a specialty in neurofeedback: Decision points. *Journal of Mental Health Counseling*, 38(2), 155–169.

Chapin, T.J. & Russell-Chapin, L.A. (2014). *Neurotherapy and neurofeedback: Brain-based treatment for psychological and behavioral problems.* New York, NY: Routledge.

Conway, E.M. (2005). Collaborative responses to the demands of emerging human needs: The role of faith and spirituality in education for social work. *Journal of Religion and Spirituality in Social Work*, 24(1/2), 65–77.

Council for Accreditation of Counseling and Related Educational Programs. (2015). *CACREP 2016 standards.* Retrieved from www.cacrep.org/wp-content/uploads/2012/10/2016-CACREP-Standards.pdf

Csiernik, R., Furze, P., Dromgole, L., & Rishchynski, G. (2006). Information technology and social work: The dark side or light side? *Journal of Evidence-Based Social Work*, 3(3/4), 9–26.

Damianakis, T., Climans, R., & Marziali, E. (2008). Social workers' experiences of virtual psychotherapeutic caregivers groups for Alzheimer's, Parkinson's, Stroke, Frontotemporal Dementia and Traumatic Brain Injury. *Social Work with Groups*, 31(2), 99–116.

Davys, A.M. & Beddoe, L. (2008). Interprofessional learning for supervision: "Taking the blinkers off." *Learning in Health & Social Care*, 8(1), 58–69.

DeShazer, S. (1985). *Keys to solution in brief therapy.* New York, NY: W.W. Norton.

Doidge, N. (2007). *The brain that changes itself.* New York, NY: Penguin Books.

Dufrene, R.L. & Tanner, Z. (2008). Multimedia CD: Play therapy counseling skills. *Journal of Technology and Counseling*, 5(1). Retrieved January 2009, from http://jtc.colstate.edu/Vol5_1/Dufrene.htm

Elliott, R. (2002). Hermeneutic single-case efficacy design. *Psychotherapy Research*, 12, 1–21.

Falender, C.A. & Shafranske, E.P. (2007). Competence in competency-based supervision practice: Construct and application. *Professional Psychology: Research & Practice*, 383(3), 232–240.

Falender, C.A. & Shafranske, E.P. (2004). *Clinical supervision: A competency-based approach.* Washington, DC: American Psychological Association.

Field, T.A., Jones, L.K., & Russell-Chapin, L.A. (Eds.). (2017). *Neurocounseling: Brain-based clinical applications.* Alexandria, VA: American Counseling Association.

Ganor, K.A. & Constantine, M.G. (2002). Multicultural group supervision: A comparison of in-person vs. Web-based formats. *Professional School Counseling*, 6, 104–121.

Haber, R., Marshall, D., Cowan, K., Vanlandingham, A., Gerson, M., & Fitch, J. (2009). "Live" supervision of supervision: "Perpendicular" interventions in parallel processes. *Clinical Supervisor*, 28(1), 72–90.

Hair, H.J. & O'Donoghue, K. (2009). Culturally relevant, socially just social work supervision: Becoming visible through a social constructivist lens. *Journal of Ethnic & Cultural Diversity in Social Work*, 18(1/2), 70–88.

Harvey, V.S. & Carlson, J.F. (2003). Ethical and professional issues with computer-related technology. *School Psychology Review*, 32, 92–104.

Hicks, M. (2009). Religious/spiritual matters not to be ignored. *The National Psychologist*, 18(1), 17.

Holloway, J.D. (2003). Professional will: A responsible thing to do. APA *Online Monitor*, 34(2). Retrieved January 2009 from www.apa.org/monitorfeb03/will.html

Kampfe, C.M. (2015). *Counseling older people: Opportunities and challenges.* Alexandria, VA: American Counseling Association.

Kennedy, A. (2008). Plugged in, turned on and wired up. *Counseling Today*, 8, 34–38.

Lambert, M.J. & Barley, D.E. (2001). Research summary on the therapeutic relationship and psychotherapy outcome. *Psychotherapy*, 38(4), 357–361.

Layne, C.M. & Hohenshil, T.H. (2005). High tech counseling: Revisited. *Journal of Counseling and Development*, 83, 222–226.

Mallen, J.J., Vogel, D.L., & Rochlen, A.B. (2005). The practical aspects of on-line counseling: Ethics, training, technology and competency. *The Counseling Psychologist*, 33, 776–818.

Manzanares, M.G., O'Halloran, T.M., McCartney, T.J., Filer, R.D., Varhely, S.C., & Calhoun, K.A. (2004). CD-Rom technology for education and support of site supervisors. *Counselor Education and Supervision*, 43(3), 220–231.

Meany-Walen, K.K., Davis-Gage, D., & Lindo, N.A. (2016). The impact of wellness-focused supervision on mental health counseling practicum students. *Journal of Counseling and Development*, 94(4), 464–472. doi.org/10.1002/jcad.12105

Norcross, J.C. (Ed.). (2011). *Psychotherapy relationships that work: Evidence-based responsiveness* (2nd ed.). New York: Oxford University Press.

Panos, P.T. (2005). A model for using videoconferencing technology to support international social work field practicum students. *International Social Work*, 48(6), 834–841.

Polling Report, The (2004). *FOX News/Opinion Dynamics Poll*, September 23–24, 2003. Retrieved January 2009 from www.pollingreport.com/religion.htm

Porges, S.W. (2011). *The polyvagal theory: Foundations of emotions, attachment, communication, and self-regulation*. New York, NY: W.W. Norton.

Ragusea, S.A. (2002). A professional living will for psychologists. In L. VandeCreek & T.L. Jackson (Eds.), *Innovations in clinical practice: A source book* (pp. 301–305). Sarasota, FL: Professional Resource Press.

Ray, D. & Altekruse, M. (2000). Effectiveness of group supervision versus combined group and individual supervision. *Counselor Education and Supervision*, 40(9), 19–30.

Reese, R.J., Usher, E.L., Bowman, D.C., Norsworthy, L.A., Halstead, J.L., Rowlands, S.R., & Chisholm, R.R. (2009). Using client feedback in psychotherapy training: An analysis of its influence on supervision and counselor self-efficacy. *Training and Education in Professional Psychology*, 3(3), 157–168.

Reisinger Walker, E., McGee, R.T., & Druss, B.G. (2015). Mortality in mental disorders and global disease burden implications. A systemic review and meta-analysis. *JAMA Psychiatry*, 72(4), 334–341. doi:10.1001/jamapsychiatry.2014.2502

Rizzo, V.M. & Rowe, J.M. (2006). Studies of the cost-effectiveness of social work services in aging: A review of the literature. *Research on Social Work Practice*, 16(1), 67–73.

Rousmaniere, T. & Frederickson, J. (2016). Remote live supervision: Videoconference for one-way-mirror supervision. In T. Rousmaniere & E. Renfro-Michel (Eds)., *Using technology to enhance clinical supervision* (pp. 157–174). Alexandria, VA: American Counseling Association. doi:10.1002/9781119268499.ch10

Russell, S.R. & Yarhouse, M.A. (2006). Religion/spirituality within APA accredited psychology predoctoral internships. *Professional Psychology: Research and Practice*, 37, 430–436.

Russell-Chapin, L.A. (2007). Supervision: An essential for professional counselor development. In J. Gregorie & C.M. Jungers (Eds.), *The counselor's companion: What every beginning counselor needs to know* (pp. 79–80). Mahwah, NJ: Lawrence Erlbaum.

Schwartz, J. and Begley, S. (2003). *The mind and the brain: Neuroplasticity and the power of mental force*. New York, NY: HarperCollins.

Shaw, H.E. & Shaw, S.F. (2006). Critical ethical issues in online counseling: Assessing current practices with an ethical intent checklist. *Journal of Counseling & Development*, 85, 41–53.

Stoltenberg, C.D. & Pace, T.M. (2008). Science and practice in supervision: An evidence-based practice in psychology approach. In W. Bruce Walsh (Ed.), *Biennial Review of Counseling Psychology*. New York, NY: Psychology Press.

Stoltenberg, C.D. & Pace, T.M. (2007). The scientist-practitioner model: Now more than ever. *Journal of Contemporary Psychotherapy*, 37, 195–203.

U.S. Department of Labor, Bureau of Labor Statistics (2014). Librarians. *Occupational outlook handbook,* 2014–2024 Edition. Retrieved from www.bls.gov/ooh/education-training-and-library/librarians.htm

U.S. Health Resources & Services Administration (2016). *National projections of supply and demand for selected behavioral health practitioners: 2013–2025.* Rockville, MD: National Center for Workforce Analysis.

Vaccaro, N. & Lambie, G.W. (2007). Computer-based counselor-in-training supervision: Ethical and practical implications for counselor educators and supervisors, *Counselor Education & Supervision,* 47(9), 46–56.

Vespa, J., Armstrong, D.M., & Medina, L. (2018). Demographic turning points for the United States: Population projections for 2020 to 2060. *Current Population Reports,* 25–1144. Washington, DC: U.S. Census Bureau.

Watson, J.C. (2005). Factors influencing the online learning efficacy beliefs of counselors in training. *Journal of Technology in Counseling,* 4(1). Retrieved January 2009, from http://jtc.colstate.edu/Vol14_1/indes.htm

Watson, J.C. (2003). Computer-based supervision: Implementing computer technology into the delivery of counseling supervision. *Journal of Technology in Counseling,* 3(1).

World Health Organization (2018). *ICD-10-CM international classification of disease,* Tenth Revision, Clinical Modification. Geneva: World Health Organization.

Young, J.S., Cashwell, C., Wiggins-Frame, M., & Belair, C. (2002). Spiritual and religious competencies: A national survey from CACREP-Accredited programs. *Counseling and Values,* 47, 22–23.

INDEX

Made in the USA
Monee, IL
19 August 2021